BAFFLED BY ADDICTION?

SUCCESSFUL STRATEGIES TO HELP YOUR ADDICTED LOVED ONE

ED HUGHES, MPS, LICDC

RONALD TURNER, MD, CDCA

GroundSwell, LLC
2465 Thomas Avenue
Portsmouth, OH 45662
www.baffledbyaddiction.com

ISBN 978-0-615-26730-2

*To Rem, Jim, Tom, Ray, and
all our other teachers...*

Contents

Introduction

More than twenty-two million Americans suffer from alcohol or other drug addictions. For each of these individuals, the disease significantly impacts at least ten other people, the majority of whom are in the affected individual's family. When the peripheral costs of addiction—health care, insurance, criminal activities—are considered, virtually no one escapes its consequences.

We live in the midst of an addiction epidemic. The victims are younger, the drugs are more powerful, and the consequences are more severe. Narcotics such as heroin, prescription pain medications, methamphetamine, and crack cocaine are used by a generation of addicted people that has spread to every community, socioeconomic level, and ethnic culture. The group that absorbs by far the largest share of the impact is the family.

This book describes a set of strategies designed to help family members help their addicted loved one efficiently and effectively. The goal is to apply the widely accepted disease concept of addiction to practical, real-life situations encountered by people whose lives have been affected by an addicted loved one. The suggested strategies provide distraught friends and family members with insightful tools to caringly steer their loved one toward abstinence and recovery. Everyone wants to do the right thing to help; this book provides the guidance to do just that.

Five years ago Ed Hughes, executive director of The Counseling Center in Portsmouth, Ohio, formed the Loved Ones Group, a continuous, seven-session education program for families impacted by addiction. At these weekly gatherings family members receive information about the disease, share common concerns, and ask questions about everything from active addiction to recovery.

The purpose of the Loved Ones Group, and now this book, is to impress on friends and family members that their addicted loved one cannot begin to get better until he experiences the consequences of his addiction, and that he will not obtain the personal motivation to seek help until the family ceases rescuing. By shedding the shrouds of secrecy and denial, families can effectively shift the consequences of the addiction from the family to the addicted individual.

Early involvement is vital. Families must become familiar with the disease of addiction regardless of their loved one's willingness to enter treatment. Thus engaged, families are able to coordinate their actions with treatment providers to increase the potential for success. Organizations such as Loved Ones Groups, Al-Anon, and community addiction treatment agencies offer opportunities to learn about the realities of addiction, relapse, and the need for long-term treatment approaches.

There is no single, accepted "right" way to approach this subject. While many treatment and recovery agendas are available, the strategies embraced here are based on what has worked best for a large number of people over a significant period of time. The concepts are based on the results of science, personal experience, successful outcomes, and common sense. Perhaps less objectively, the suggestions also arise from years of caring about addicted loved ones and their families.

The first section of the book identifies the problem of addiction and discusses the role of the family. Family members, by not rescuing their addicted loved one from the consequences caused by his addiction, have the power to provide a solution. Section Two describes in detail ten strategies, or goals, available to families that can result in their loved one asking for help. Chapter 1 of this section provides the basis for understanding that addiction is a disease; disease stages and common myths are also addressed. The core message, "Don't rescue," appears in Chapter 2, and is supported by examples of its effectiveness. Chapters 3 through 8 supply families with specific avoidance strategies when interacting with the disease. Chapter 9 reveals the joys and heartaches of the recovery process, and Chapter 10 emphasizes the need to reclaim one's own life. Extending beyond the immediacy of the addicted loved one, the last section provides suggestions for helpful community-based activities.

The Appendices provide additional valuable material, including addiction symptom checklists, the outlined strategies, more detailed drug information, and suggested readings and resources.

For easier reading, the authors adopted the male "he" and "his" throughout as the default gender. This should not be interpreted as gender bias; we are acutely aware that females are equally affected by addiction. Our effort was only to avoid the awkward "his or her" or (worse) "he/she" constructions and thereby streamline the text. We also chose to use "addicted person" or "addicted individual" instead of the stigmatizing term "addict." And because alcohol is a drug just like any other, the terms "addiction" and "drug addiction" refer to the obsessive use of any addictive substance, including alcohol.

Though one measure of a book's success is sales, our yardstick is the number of addicted loved ones who find recovery because of their family's application of the principles espoused in these pages. This material is intended to provide insight into the often bizarre behavior of your loved one's thinking. To refrain from rescuing your loved one from the consequences created by his addiction will be one of the most painful—and most loving—tasks that you will ever have to experience. Having personally felt your pain, we hope this small book will provide some measure of guidance and support during the process of helping your loved one save his life.

Ed Hughes
Ron Turner

Preface

I have been working in and around the addiction field for twenty-six years, including the past eighteen years as director of a comprehensive addiction treatment program. Prior to my professional work I too suffered from addiction in the form of alcoholism, but I was fortunate. I was introduced to recovery at the early age of twenty-eight by a group of helpful and loving people, some of whom were professional alcoholism counselors.

Over the years I have learned much from my own recovery experience, but even more from the recovery stories of others. I was initially influenced by a treatise written by James Milam, Ph.D., *The Emergent Comprehensive Concept of Alcoholism*, and later by his book, *Under the Influence*. Milam's presentation of addiction as a disease was one of those moments of enlightenment offered by people who have either worked vigorously in the field of addiction or have won my heart through their struggles toward recovery.

We have long known that families can play a vital role in the recovery of their loved ones, but we were at a loss when it actually came to involving family members, friends, and employers. My agency was no different; we lacked family input, cooperation, and influence.

Then one evening over dinner my wife Kendra, who for many years has been active in groups that help family members with addicted loved ones, confronted me in a way that only she can: "Ed, there are parents, spouses, and grandparents in our community who need help in dealing with their loved one's addiction. You've got to do something."

That conversation led to the formation of our first Loved Ones Group, an educational and support program for families who were worrying themselves to death over the condition of a loved one. Hundreds of concerned people have since come through the group, and many addicted loved ones have found their way to recovery as a result of the strategies their family members learned by attending. We now have three Loved Ones Groups in southern Ohio.

The idea for this book came from my best friend, Dr. Ron Turner, who has also shared the vision of helping families and loved ones for a long time. Ron, a published writer, has lent his expertise in addiction, writing, and editing to this work, a pursuit that never would have happened without his skill and encouragement.

Some of the information I will be sharing with you is based on the most recent research in the field of addiction, much comes from my own experience, and even more comes from what I have been taught by families and individuals suffering from addiction. Many of my suggestions will seem difficult and perhaps harsh when you first read them. Please remember that although this book is meant for family members, my goal is to help your loved one through you. I believe strongly in the potential for your loved one's recovery and your ability to reclaim the relationship that you so much desire.

We have a saying at my agency: "We don't believe in miracles; we rely upon them." This miracle needs your help, and what I will be asking you to do for your loved one will be one the hardest things you have ever attempted. I will be asking you for a demonstration of love that few parents, spouses, or friends have ever been asked to make.

Ed Hughes, 2009

SECTION ONE:

DEFINING THE PROBLEM

Defining the Problem

If you suspect that your loved one—your child, spouse, parent, sibling, or good friend—has a drinking or other drug problem you're probably correct. Your concern alone is a powerful indicator that a problem exists.

It's important to view addiction in the context of a disease that affects millions of people. And for each addicted person there are millions more who are directly or indirectly impacted by the disease. Family members, friends, coworkers, and employers are all affected. Monetary considerations aside, addiction is a disease with symptoms that produce powerful emotional responses from those in contact with the addicted individual.

Addiction is every family member's worst nightmare. Because of the deep-seated stigma historically associated with alcoholism and drug addiction, families are hesitant to ask for help. The first hurdles that any family must overcome are the shame and guilt associated with having an addicted person as a family member. Historically the causes of alcoholism and drug addiction have been erroneously blamed on character weakness, lack of willpower, immorality, and the environment in which the person lives or grew up. When addiction is not viewed as a disease both the addicted person and the family become guilt-ridden and secretive. With no other disease do the people involved feel shame of such magnitude.

Addiction produces a series of crises of ever-increasing intensity. Rescuing the addicted individual from any given crisis guarantees that another, greater crisis will occur. The sequence may begin with some small theft from the family, such as money from Mom's purse, or obtaining money from a family member under false pretenses. Since family members are rarely aware of any drug use at this stage, consequences are usually averted. But since addiction is involved, these activities will intensify: a DUI (driving under the influence), misuse of a credit card, or direct theft from another family member will follow.

Then if you, instead of your loved one, pay the court costs or make reparations, he'll experience no consequences due to his drug or alcohol use. Only when you become willing to stop solving the problems created by your loved one's disease will he face the consequences that lead to a personal turning point—a place where he'll find his own compelling reason to accept help.

Most assuredly your loved one's consequences will continue to increase in both frequency and magnitude until they reach a point beyond the family's ability or willingness to solve them. *Willingness* is the key. Once you become willing to stop solving the problems created by your loved one's disease, he'll reach a personal turning point—a place where he'll accept help. Only then can recovery begin. So the earlier the cessation of rescuing, the fewer and milder the consequences. You'll be hearing this refrain repeatedly throughout this book: *the addicted person's turning point is always a crisis beyond the family's ability or willingness to fix it.*

The necessary change involves removing the safety net that you've been providing for your loved one.

This safety net gives him a sense of security and makes him immune from the consequences he's creating. When the safety net is removed your loved one will experience the full magnitude of his disease, which includes a sense of continuing and progressive calamity that so far has been shouldered by the family. Without a safety net his drug use will be different: he'll experience not only the euphoria of the drug but also the potential reality of its consequences. Always keep in mind that the addicted person must actually experience and feel the consequences—the effects of his disease—before he reaches his turning point and asks for help.

The ultimate aim in helping your addicted loved one is to get all family members to change, to become willing to cease rescuing. The process begins when just one person finally says, "This isn't working. Let's try something else. Let's let the consequences play out." However, while it is rare for all family members to come to agreement on the right course of action at the same time, significant progress can be realized if even one family member takes effective action.

Since this new approach is rarely accepted by all family members immediately, the first one who tries to deal with the disease more effectively is often misunderstood by the others and may be accused of withdrawing help from the loved one: "You don't care about him anymore!" As we will discuss later, all family members are affected in various ways by the loved one's addiction.

In this book we use the expression "hitting bottom" to refer to the designation typically used by those who have reached a turning point and are recovering from the disease of addiction. This phrase, however, often carries a negative connotation that suggests that no one recovers until having lived through the very worst the disease has to offer. Actually, "bottom" simply represents that moment in time when an addicted person experiences consequences that lead him to consider asking for help. Bottoms are different for each recovering person and vary widely in the depth and breadth of the suffering. A fundamental goal of this book is to help families "raise the bottom" for their loved ones. In so doing, the intensity of the bottom is lessened, which helps the loved one avoid any harsher penalties of addiction.

(At this early stage in your investigation, you may want to refer to Appendix A: Symptom Checklist for specific questions to ask yourself when trying to determine if your loved one has a problem with alcohol or drugs.)

The section that follows consists of "Ten Strategies to Help Your Addicted Loved One." Achieving a successful outcome, like any process, will take time; immediate, overnight results rarely occur. And since family members are as powerless over the addicted person as the addicted person is over his drug, some false starts and temporary setbacks are to be expected. The ten strategies should be viewed as individual goals and approached separately to obtain the tools necessary to help your addicted loved one.

SECTION TWO:

TEN STRATEGIES TO HELP
YOUR ADDICTED LOVED ONE

1) Learn All You Can About the Disease of Addiction

Addiction Is a Disease

Conditions known to be diseases, such as diabetes, rheumatoid arthritis, and cancer, have certain characteristics in common. These include:

- known causative or precipitating factors
- a unique set of symptoms
- specific diagnostic criteria
- reinforcing laboratory data
- a predictable course
- accepted treatment regimens

Realizing that addiction shares these same attributes makes acceptance of your loved one's condition as a disease of the body, rather than a character flaw or a result of his environment, that much easier. The sections that follow expand on the disease concept of addiction, a vitally important concept when applying the suggested strategies.

Only when we understand the characteristics and dynamics of addiction can we begin to respond effectively to its symptoms. Realizing that addiction is a progressive disease allows us to understand that *addicted individuals are sick people who need to get well, not bad people who need to become good.*

> Expert Definitions

Perhaps most comprehensive is the definition given by Nora Volkov, MD, director of the National Institute on Drug Abuse (NIDA): "Addiction is a disease of the brain that translates into abnormal behavior."

An early depiction of the disease concept of addiction appeared in James Milam's 1974 publication, *The Emergent Comprehensive Concept of Alcoholism*. Milam proposed that addiction is a disease of the body and not a self-induced condition, a reaction to soured environmental situations, or a medicating of mental health problems. Instead he indicated that addiction is a primary, chronic, progressive disease rooted in the physical differences in the way drugs are metabolized by addicted people compared to the general population.

Definitions of addiction with a home-spun feel offered by other respected researchers in the field of addiction can be helpful. Mark Willenbring, MD, director of Treatment and Recovery with the National Institute on Alcohol Abuse and Alcoholism (NIAAA) calls addiction "wanting the wrong thing very, very badly."

Kathleen Brady, MD, PhD, professor of psychiatry at the Medical School of the University South Carolina and an expert in addiction and co-occurring psychiatric disorders, describes addiction as "the compulsive use of a drug...that interferes with the ability to function in multiple ways." And Joseph Frascella, PhD, chief of the Etiology and Clinical Neurobiology Branch at NIDA, says that "addictions are repetitive behaviors in the face of negative consequences, the desire to continue something you know is bad for you."

Becoming Addicted

Drug surveys indicate that over ninety percent of the people in the United States have tried alcohol and nearly fifty percent have experimented with an illegal drug. But we know that ninety percent of Americans are not alcoholic and fifty percent are not drug-addicted. The statistical reality is that out of a hundred people who smoke a cigarette, eighty-five will become addicted to nicotine (making nicotine the most addictive of all drugs). Out of a hundred people who take a drink of alcohol, fifteen will become alcoholic. For most opiate-based drugs, the number is about thirty, and for crack cocaine it's close to sixty.

Every day thousands of individuals are introduced to an addictive drug for the first time, and the reasons for doing so vary widely. An eighth-grader sneaks his first cigarette; a teenager drinks his first beer; a post-op patient takes his first opiate-based painkiller; a party-goer experiments with marijuana; or an elderly insomniac tries a tranquilizer to help him sleep. No matter what the precise scenario, however, no one takes that first drink or drug with the intention of becoming addicted. The *reason* for the initial contact is irrelevant.

Historically, society has been obsessed with determining the cause of, or blame for, the addicted person's first encounter with an addictive substance. Was it peer pressure, an effort to escape, or just curiosity? Perhaps the first drink was due to stress or fear, or an attempt to erase a bad memory. Or was it because the individual grew up around people who drank or used drugs? Yet if these are valid explanations for an addicted person's addiction, why didn't the millions of other people who experimented under the same circumstances also become addicted? So again, the *reason* for taking the first drink or drug does not determine whether or not a certain individual will become addicted.

So what sets your loved one apart? Why did he become addicted? As we shall see in *The Myths of Addiction* below, neither he nor the family are to blame. He didn't become addicted because he was stupid, reckless, mentally ill, depressed, anxious, unfortunate in love, or outwardly different. And he didn't become addicted because of his environment, neighborhood, or family. These explanations may seem superficially attractive, but when held up to the scrutiny of science or even common sense, they fall short.

Although there are certain circumstances that make it more likely that an individual will experiment with alcohol or drugs, the only differing determinant is within that person's body. *The primary reason that certain people become addicted (and others do not) is that their body metabolizes the drug in a way that produces a heightened pleasurable experience far greater than that obtained by those who do not become addicted.*

This abnormal, powerful experience initiates a progressive attraction to the drug, which in turn further affects the basic physiology of the person's brain. This altered brain function eventually results in a progression of significant behavioral and social

24

consequences which, in turn, complement and encourage the continued attraction to the drug. So a person's addiction is no one's fault and no one's to blame. Not the family, an unsavory peer group, or the stress of life. Not even the addicted person himself.

In some cases it's possible to become addicted to drugs without the concomitant abnormally heightened euphoria, such as with individuals for whom addictive drugs have been continuously prescribed for health reasons. Most people, when exposed to addictive drugs for a long period, will experience withdrawal symptoms when they try to reduce their dosage or quit and will feel a need for more of the drug to avoid those symptoms. We see many people who have become addicted after receiving either opiate-based painkillers (such as Oxycontin, Percodan, or Vicodin) or benzodiazepines (such as Valium, Xanex or Ativan) for extended periods.

Addiction as a Side Effect

That the majority of people experiment with alcohol or another drug at least once during their lives is undisputed. As mentioned, over ninety percent will try alcohol and over fifty percent will try an illegal drug, including underage alcohol. Yet the prevalence of alcoholism and drug addiction is far below these rates. Only a minority of experimenters experience the addictive "side effect" of drug consumption.

To give an analogy, pharmaceutical television commercials usually begin with a list of symptoms, name the drug that alleviates those symptoms, and finish with a rapid-fire inventory of possible side effects. To be rid of your runny nose and watery eyes you might also have to put up with a rash, insomnia, or temporary loss of sexual performance. While very few consumers will note any side effects, a small percentage will experience an abnormal reaction because their body chemistry is different. Compared to the unaffected majority, this minority came from similar homes, exhibited the same amount of willpower, and was under no greater stress. They experienced the side effects because their bodies were different.

The same is true for your loved one who is struggling with an addictive substance. When he first experimented with alcohol or another drug as the majority of people do, he was among the minority who experienced a side effect. The side effect for him was an intensely powerful response—the WOW response—that compelled him to seek that response again and again.

Your loved one experienced the side effect of a drug because of a difference in his body chemistry. That difference led to compulsive use. It was not caused by mental illness, stress, or any other outside influence. No one is at fault so no one is to blame.

If you were to ask your loved one (if you haven't already), "Why do you drink the way you do?" or "How can you take all those drugs?" you would receive a misleading, defensive answer of denial or anger. His true thoughts would reveal that he, too, is mystified: "Why don't you drink the way I do?" or "How can you resist these wonderful, mind-changing drugs?" Your addicted loved one is obtaining an experience from a drug that is entirely different from your experience. Being unaware of the physical differences, both you and your loved one conclude that the abnormal drinking or drug use is because he's bad, immoral, weak-willed, hopeless, or a little insane. At this point neither of you can explain it any other way.

The Myths of Addiction

Be forewarned: most of the opinions you will hear about addiction are wrong. Instead of being swayed by obsolete beliefs that claim that only willpower is necessary to quit, challenge these out-of-date ideas with solid, new information.

> ➢ *Weak Moral Character*

Though commonly believed by the general public as well as misguided professionals, addicted people are no more flawed prior to initiating their disease than the general population. The personality characteristics of addicted individuals are completely representative of the variations found in all groups of people. Some are smart, some are not so smart; some are right-handed, some are left-handed; some are mentally ill, most are not.

A recovering person had this recollection:

> I previously believed that "not fitting in" was a cause of my own addiction. Then, at my twentieth high school reunion, I heard some of my old friends, a group of non-addicted women, describing their high school experience as a time when they "didn't fit in." I finally realized that

27

"not fitting in" was a characteristic not
of addiction but of adolescence.

Since so many addictions begin during adolescence
it's not uncommon to link the experiences together.

➤ *Stress or Traumatic Events*

Like the country song says, "My wife left me so I
started drinking." In all likelihood, the fella was
drinking before she left and she left because of his
drinking. If difficult life events caused addiction, we'd
all be addicted.

There is a relationship between life's stresses and
addiction, but it's not a causal one. Think of stress as
pain. Our primitive brains approach pain very simply:
once experienced, avoid it.

The addicted person's brain responds differently to
stress. Instead of avoiding the pain, the solution is to
take a drink or drug. While drinking or drug use
doesn't solve problems for normal people, it often
provides significant, albeit short-term, relief for
addicted individuals.

And this is where things get complicated. While
the drug seemingly alleviates a difficulty, it simultaneously creates more problems. The addicted
brain's response to these new problems remains
unchanged: take more of the drug. And since the
original difficulty was only masked and never solved,
the addicted person begins "collecting" problems. As
these unresolved conflicts accumulate over the years,
an enormous amount of stress develops. And the
solution for these accumulated problems is again the
same: take more of the drug.

Now add to this the pain of withdrawal. For nearly all addicted people, withdrawal is experienced for three primary reasons: inaccessibility of the drug (including lack of money), attempts to control its use, and increased tolerance to the drug. The drug dealer may mysteriously disappear or the friendly doctor may stop writing prescriptions. An employer or family member may bring pressure to stop using, which may postpone the drug use. Increased tolerance means that more of the drug is needed more frequently to thwart the physical effects of withdrawal. This, of course, prompts even greater usage.

The process of "collecting" unresolved problems resembles a mounting debt that will have to be paid eventually. Because this repayment often begins once sobriety is achieved, it's not uncommon for the newly recovering person to be overwhelmed by the emotional conflicts and monetary issues that have accumulated during years of drinking or drug use. Professional guidance in handling these problems is another reason why treatment during early recovery is essential.

And what should the family do to help resolve these past-due problems? In a word, nothing. It's important that family members refrain once again from rescuing. Not only will any such effort likely fail but direct support at this point will actually reduce the motivation to recover.

➤ *Weak Willpower*

Another common misconception is that addicted people lack willpower. In fact, addicted individuals possess the same amount of willpower as the general population: some have a great deal and some seem to be lacking altogether. Ironically, as the disease of addiction progresses, the addicted person must exert extreme levels of willpower just to accomplish otherwise normal tasks.

Stories from recovering individuals reveal in some measure how much effort was required just to "survive"—to get up in the morning, make breakfast for the kids, go to work, and stay at work. The motivation stems from the addicted person's attempts to control his use and make his behavior seem normal. While willpower exerted in this manner might temporarily slow the progression of the disease, even monumental efforts are almost always doomed. Just as willpower alone cannot overcome cancer or diabetes or diarrhea, willpower is no match for the power of addiction.

The excessive willpower demonstrated during the active phase of addiction sometimes persists well into sobriety. Many individuals in recovery have accomplished goals they once thought were unattainable. In these instances willpower actually seems to have gained strength during the course of the disease.

> *Addictive Personality*

When researchers began studying the personalities of addicted individuals, they discovered many shared characteristics. They found them to be compulsive, irresponsible, moody, self-centered, lacking in insight, possessing low self-esteem, immature, emotionally hypersensitive, and frequently irrational, dishonest, and manipulative. They were likely to use multiple substances, and to indulge in cigarettes and coffee.

These investigations and their conclusions, however, represent yet another example of the upside down thinking prevalent in the area of addiction. The studies were flawed because the addicted individuals were analyzed *after* their addictions had become active. The traits that these professionals ascribed to the addictive personality were actually *symptoms* of the disease. By erroneously assuming that these characteristics were present prior to the onset of drug use, they presumed that the addicted person was predisposed to becoming addicted. Cause and effect were reversed.

Prior to beginning drug use, the personalities of addicted people reflect the same heterogeneous variances found in the general population. It's the disease that causes the similar personality changes— the *symptoms* of the disease—which in turn make the personalities of addicted people appear similar. (For further information, see *The Addictive Personality,* by Craig Nakken, in Appendix D: Resources, Texts.)

➤ *Environment*

Many addicted individuals come from homes where addiction was present which, to some, indicates that environmental factors, such as drug or alcohol availability and social acceptance, are the root causes of addiction. This is to overlook the genetic component of addiction. For example, the male offspring of alcoholic fathers have an incidence of the disease four times greater than children of nonalcoholic fathers. And children of nonalcoholic parents have comparatively low rates of alcoholism, even when raised by alcoholic foster parents. Ongoing studies continue to reveal differences in the genetic makeup of people with addiction. The disease of addiction is fundamentally a product of genetics and not of a specific environment.

Environment can, however, play a role in the timing of the onset of the disease. Some home and community environments offer an opportunity for early experimentation and some are more tolerant of the negative behaviors created by drug use. For example, parents who use drugs are less likely to monitor or educate their children about the potential harm of use. Neighborhoods infested with illicit drugs also increase the risk of early experimentation, especially with highly addictive drugs. Yet while environment does not *cause* the disease, certain high-risk surroundings create opportunities for early use and promote an attitude of drinking or drug use acceptability.

> *Low Self-Esteem*

Another example of upside down thinking is that low self-esteem either causes addiction or makes the individual more vulnerable to addiction. Prior to the onset of the disease, before experimentation with that first drink or drug, the self-esteem of people with addiction varies just as it does for people in general. Some have high self-esteem, some have low self-esteem, and most fall somewhere in the middle. As the addiction progresses, however, any amount of self-esteem takes a serious beating.

The addicted person learns that drugs can act as a short-term "fix" in dealing with most normal human difficulties. Not only can they alleviate depression, sorrow, disappointment, loneliness and anxiety, they can even improve on otherwise positive experiences. The distressing result, of course, is that the addicted person, instead of learning important social and emotional skills, has ceased to mature: he has stopped growing up. And in time the emotional stunting is revealed in debilitating personality traits.

A Foundation For Change

Realizing that addiction is a disease provides the foundation for a necessary change. Previous notions that drug or alcohol addiction is due to a character defect can be set aside and allow the family to see and respond to the addicted person differently. We know that rescuing leads inevitably to yet another crisis. By accepting that addiction is a progressive disease, one that is arrested only when the addicted person is motivated to change by his consequences, family members can find the strength to stop rescuing.

Viewing addiction as a disease also helps family members change their perception of their loved one's behavior. Instead of seeing his uncharacteristic, unattractive actions as products of a "bad" person, they are understood instead to be symptoms of a disease, thereby adding an element of predictability. Most certainly your loved one lied to you; without a doubt he acted irresponsibly. But dishonesty and irresponsibility are only symptoms of the disease of addiction.

Beneath each family member's anger and shame toward the addicted loved one lies the unrealistic expectation that today will be different, that this time he will keep his promise, do the right thing, and change for the better. Without recovery, however, your loved one will continue to display the symptoms of his disease, which promise, over time, to become more complicated, pervasive, and unattractive.

The earlier the disease is recognized and the earlier the addicted person seeks treatment, the greater is his chance for complete recovery. Historically, alcoholism and drug addiction were defined by their later stages: "An alcoholic or addict is an individual who drinks or uses drugs every day, has lost everything, is homeless and living under a bridge, and carries a bottle in a brown paper sack." Indeed, this person probably is alcoholic or addicted. But did this person always look that way? Of course not. He easily could have once had a job, family, hopes, and dreams. In fact, most addicted people never reach the "rock bottom" that typically defines the disease of addiction.

The goal, then, is to identify and respond to the disease before it reaches this stage. The definition of "addict" must change. Understanding that the disease of addiction begins slowly and subtly and has been present long before one loses all his material possessions means acknowledging that recovery can—and should—begin much earlier. The disease cannot be confronted until the revised definition of addict is understood and the bottom has been raised.

The shame that permeates addiction prevents families from discovering that their loved one suffers from the same symptoms, behaviors, and disappointments as all other addicted individuals. Once families understand that the lying, stealing, manipulating, and breaking promises are universal symptoms of the disease of addiction, they will begin to make more appropriate decisions when interacting with their loved one. The self-centeredness and selfishness that epitomize the addicted person's personality present barriers to the family unless they accept that the disease itself is at the root of the behaviors. And unless the disease is thwarted, the behaviors will only worsen.

Our primitive brain is always at work trying to alleviate our discomfort, pain, and cravings. Put your hand on a hot stove and the brain instructs you to take it off. Start to put your hand back on the stove and the brain says stop: the brain is learning.

But what happens when the brain is faced with addiction and its consequences? Does the brain say "stop" to using drugs? No, it says just the opposite. When a progressing addicted person experiences a disappointment, such as loss of a job loss, or some direct consequence of drinking, such as a hangover, the addicted person's brain says "drink" or "use," even when the event was precipitated by drinking or using.

Progression of Addiction

When left untreated the disease of addiction, like so many other conditions, progressively gets worse. Until recently, addiction was not generally diagnosed until it had reached its late stages. By then the addicted person was perhaps living under a bridge, unemployable, and unable to care for himself. Imagine if people were unwilling to call a condition "cancer" until the patient had wasted away to nothing, or if we didn't diagnose diabetes until a limb had been removed or eyesight had been lost.

By utilizing a new definition of addiction and by identifying the symptoms of the disease in its earlier stages, families can apply the strategies necessary to get their addicted loved one into treatment much sooner. By doing so, not only are the chances for success much greater, but less money is wasted and fewer are hours spent agonizing.

To loved ones looking on, the progression of the disease of addiction is actually a progression of crises. The current crisis is only "today's" crisis. After each crisis there's often a honeymoon period when tempers cool and apologies are made...until the next crisis. Like a free-falling elevator picking up speed during its descent, the crises continue to increase in both frequency and magnitude.

Alcoholics Anonymous accurately describes alcoholism as "cunning, baffling, and powerful." The disease rarely follows a predictable, uninterrupted course from onset to complete deterioration. The addicted person will often improve for a period of time when things seem to be better or even under control. There may even be intervals of complete abstinence. Each of these rally points, however, is inevitably followed by a new crisis that leaves the addicted person worse than before. For the family, maintaining a valid perspective becomes extremely difficult. Like being in the eye of a hurricane, the calmness distracts from the whirling storm nearby.

Stages of Addiction

Addiction is often broken down into three basic stages based on the duration of the addiction, the emotional and physical impact of the drug, and the addicted person's psychological and physical response to the chemical.

These broad stages are used to categorize the phases of addiction but individual variations are common. And while addiction is not directly caused by low self-esteem, depression, anxiety, stress, or life circumstances, each plays a role in the manner in which the disease progresses.

So the rate of progression varies among individuals and even within the individual. As mentioned, there are often periods of apparent improvement when the addicted person seems to be in control, at least temporarily. The addicted person may change drugs, switching from narcotics to alcohol in an attempt to show that he's not really addicted. There may also be an interval, jokingly called the "marijuana maintenance program," during which the addicted person gives up everything except pot. There exist numerous variations on the theme of trying to control drug use with the use of another drug, or by altering behavior in some way to magically establish control.

➢ *Early Stage*

The early stage of addiction includes:

- *the WOW response*
- *brain chemistry changes*
- *early tolerance*
- *establishing a relationship with the drug*
- *personality changes*
- *emergence of denial*
- *family secrets*

- *story of blame*
- *world view distortion*

Physiological Manifestations

Addiction begins when a physiologically predisposed person takes a drink or uses a drug for the first time. During a period of experimentation, the *WOW response*, which brings excessive pleasure and is inherent to the susceptible individual, immediately captivates his interest.

All people are naturally attracted to their own WOW experiences, such as food, sex, falling in love, hobbies, or employment. They dedicate parts of their lives to these positive, rewarding pursuits. Yet on a WOW scale, they don't measure up to the attraction produced by addictive chemicals in the brains of certain individuals.

For the addicted person, the chemically induced WOW is enjoyable, intense, and seductive. "I loved it!" and "It was awesome!" are typical responses from an addicted person after being introduced to alcohol or a drug.

One recovering person said this about his first experience with alcohol:

> I drank more than my friends and I loved it. It was the best feeling I ever had. Afterwards I got so sick I thought I was going to die but I drank again as soon as I got another opportunity.

You'll rarely hear this kind of description from normal drinkers. They don't "love it" with such passion and they don't look forward to the next opportunity, especially after getting sick. Yet the addicted person is willing to suffer the consequences because of the intensity of the drug-induced WOW response.

Many of the events that follow the WOW experience are normal human reactions. When someone encounters a powerfully positive event, whether it's falling in love, the discovery of a new hobby, or the first sight of a newborn child, the person will be intensely attracted to that experience and will want to replicate it as soon as possible or appropriate. The goal of most people is to keep such experiences within the context of other activities and priorities of life. Someone who discovers a love for sky-diving, for example, will generally not pursue that hobby to the detriment of job or family.

And for most people who are predisposed to addiction, the first drug use does not lead them to reject all of life's other pleasurable activities. The initial idea for most is that the use of the drug is wonderful, but it must be controlled and not allowed to interfere with life in general. Unfortunately, as we now know, controlling the use of the drug is not possible for predisposed people. Despite their best efforts and application of all the willpower at their disposal, they won't be able to control the progression of their use and its ultimate destruction of their lives.

As the disease progresses, the addicted person's brain becomes less able to produce its own *pleasure-producing chemicals*. His brain's pleasure centers become dependent instead upon drugs for stimulation.

And as the brain's own chemicals continue to be depleted, more drugs are needed for stimulation. The vicious cycle continues until pleasure depends entirely on the use of drugs.

This situation progresses until, in the late stage of the disease, the addicted person needs the drug just to feel normal. In one sense he's "brain dead"—his brain has ceased to produce any naturally occurring, pleasure-producing chemicals. So in the early stage of addiction, the addicted individual "lives to use" and in the late stage he "uses to live."

Another physical phenomenon that occurs with addiction is drug *tolerance*. With time, your loved one will need greater amounts of the drug to obtain the same high he experienced with his initial use. Somehow the body learns to metabolize the drug more efficiently, which means that more is necessary to produce the same results. The need for the drug is prompted by cravings and painful withdrawal symptoms that occur with increasing frequency and severity.

Psychosocial Manifestations

During the early stage the addicted person attempts to establish a *relationship* with his favorite chemical. He's had the WOW experience several times, and he likes it. His effort now is to fit the chemical into his otherwise normal life. When he discovers that that isn't always possible, he seeks out friends and activities that allow him to maintain this new relationship.

Did your relationships with other people remain the same when you fell in love with someone? No, they took a back seat to the new relationship. Once that special "someone" came into your life your current friends and family were suddenly ranked lower in importance. The same is true for the person who has started up a new relationship with a chemical. His other relationships, while still hanging on, are placed in a position of lesser importance.

A recovering person described what occurred after her initial foray into drug use:

> I see now that I fell in love with the drug. The drug told me that I could continue my relationship with my parents, my siblings, and my boyfriend. It told me I could continue to pursue my college education and my career. But it turned out that addiction was a jealous lover. In the end it would not share me with anyone or anything and one by one I lost everything else that was important to me, leaving me with only the drug.

As the addiction progresses, the family begins to notice the appearance of subtle *personality changes*. The addicted person has new friends, he's secretive, and he's uncharacteristically selfish. Family members sense that something is changing, but they're uncertain as to the cause. There's less communication, more family conflict, and fewer hours spent as a family. If they begin to suspect that drugs or alcohol might be involved, a formidable barrier to the truth makes its appearance: *denial*.

Denial is a human experience not unique to addicted individuals. As human beings we are resistant to information that conflicts with what we want to be true. Did you once have a boyfriend or girlfriend of whom your parents didn't approve? It's highly unlikely that you reacted by saying, "You've always been such wise and generous parents so if you think this person is wrong for me I'll end the relationship immediately." More likely you argued, defended your choice, and told them they didn't know what they were talking about. Or, if you were afraid to argue, you probably voiced agreement and then went about seeing your sweetheart secretly.

Have you ever gone to the store, bought something too expensive, and then spent the entire time driving home explaining to yourself why it was OK? Everyone rationalizes or justifies and this same principle is at work when your loved one forms a relationship with a drug. His mind defends that which makes him feel good. The cost in terms of time, money, and relationships is rationalized to allow the co-existence of the drug use.

As with the addicted loved one, the family is also unable to recognize that drugs are the cause of any problems. For a considerable period, family members will continue to insist that the blame for the changes they are witnessing in their loved one lies with other people and events.

Yet even when the family finally admits that drugs may be part of the problem, it's kept a *secret*. The disgrace brought on by a disease thought to be a sin or character flaw is just too much. Ironically, the disease of addiction loves secrets; it depends on secrets for its existence. As the denial process progresses right along with the disease, so do the webs of secrecy, blame, rationalization, and justification keep on enlarging.

From the very beginning of the addicted person's use, a *story of blame* will develop and expand over time. The story proposes that the bad things that are happening in his life are beyond his control. The addicted person points to childhood events, problems with employers, or just bad luck as reasons for life not unfolding in his favor. The denial process prevents him from seeing how misguided decisions due to drug use have impacted his life.

Unfortunately, not only will family members believe this story, but they will embellish it by eagerly blaming other people and events for their loved one's problems. "My son didn't have a drug problem until he started hanging out with those other guys." Or the story may place blame directly on the family which, in turn, produces guilt. "Where did we go wrong?"

Another change that occurs during the early stage involves your loved one's mind. Once his brain has been exposed to a powerful, drug-induced high, his *world view changes* and he does not look upon anyone or anything in quite the same way. Addicted individuals often describe their drug encounters as "spiritual," meaning they were changed by the experience. Unfortunately, the primary effect of the experience is to remove the interest and joy from normal life events. Routine daily activities lose their luster; everything seems boring in comparison to the effects produced by the drug. The normal activities of life, over time, will become tasks and chores, and may eventually fall by the wayside entirely.

> *Middle Stage*

Characteristics of the middle stage of addiction include:

- *increased tolerance*
- *withdrawal*
- *appearance of problems*
- *rescuing*
- *role/relationship regression*
- *boundary crossing*
- *extreme denial*
- *triangulation*
- *maturation cessation*
- *joylessness*
- *powerlessness*

Physiological Manifestations

As the frequency and amount of usage increases, so does *tolerance* to the drug continue to progress during the middle stage. Increasing amounts of the drug are necessary to prevent intense cravings and withdrawal symptoms. In the early stage there was an emotional desire for the WOW experience but now there's a physical demand for the drug itself. More of the drug is needed to reach a high.

Also during the middle stage the addicted person begins to experience significant symptoms of *withdrawal*. Tremors, sweating, nausea, and agitation interfere with daily activities. Hangovers after excessive alcohol intake result in an inability to concentrate. Cravings begin to control the frequency of use. It is common for the addicted person to make a secret effort to control his use of the drug without the help of others or the family's knowledge.

Psychosocial Manifestations

The middle stage of addiction is ushered in by the *appearance of problems.* The difficulties may be financial, legal, family, social, health, or even mental health concerns. Common middle stage problems include:

- Financial: credit card debt, overdue rent, over-drawn checking account

- Legal: DUI, theft from family

- Family: frequent conflicts

- Social: new drinking or drug-using friends and activities

- Health: hangovers, missing work

- Mental health: depression, anxiety, boredom; blaming unhappiness on external factors, such as job, family, or stress

The addicted person's initial response to the problems is significantly influenced by his drug use. We use the term "alcologic," a tainted thinking that concludes that life's problems are causing the drug use, instead of the obvious opposite. As the problems accumulate, more chemical is used to offset the problems, which in turn causes more problems. For the addicted person the use of the drug does provide temporary relief from stress, worry, fear, depression, and anxiety. As the problems created by addiction increase then so does the use of the drug as a "helping" response to these problems: a vicious cycle.

Most often the family accepts this alcologic and begins *rescuing*. Family members feel they must fix the problem, protect their loved one, and rescue him whenever necessary. This normal initial reaction, however, ignites the unhelpful behaviors that are the subject of the remainder of this book. *Rescuing, we will discover, only guarantees that another, more serious crisis will occur.*

It's normal and desirable for parents to have a *role* with a child. While the primary role is to provide food, shelter, and money, parents also assist in developing a child's work ethic, morality, values, and attitudes. But, as all parents know, one's ability to impact these areas diminishes as the child moves into adulthood. It's clear that a parent is ineffective when attempting to "parent" an adult child.

So with an adult child, the role should normally progress to a *relationship* where there is more interplay, like friend-to-friend or brother-to-brother. When addiction is present parents get stuck in the parenting role, a role inappropriate for the age of the child.

The role can assume any number of identities but usually involves a type of caretaking that includes paying bills, rescuing from jams, making excuses for the addicted person's behavior, protecting from criticism, taking the addicted person's side in conflicts with other family members, or thwarting outside threats such as law enforcement. Some family members find themselves becoming the addicted person's brain, doing his planning, worrying, and reminding. They do everything possible to make the loved one's life appear normal. And as this role increases, there is less and less opportunity for a normal, evolving relationship.

When a mother called to ask for advice about her son, her initial description made him sound like a typical teenager. It turned out that he was forty-two years old. The mother had become "stuck in time" and her emotional connection with her son had regressed. The family member who behaves and feels as if their loved one is still a child is easily manipulated by the addiction. Rescuing and other tasks not normally associated with an adult-adult relationship become commonplace.

So the roles must end and the action to be taken is essentially inaction. "I'm not going to give you money anymore." "I'm not going to stay up all night listening." The addicted person's consequences will continue to increase in both frequency and magnitude until a consequence is reached that's beyond the family's willingness or ability to solve. Only when this occurs can recovery begin. And the earlier the family's roles of rescuing are dropped, the smaller the consequences and the sooner the door to recovery will open.

As the addiction progresses, both the addicted person and family slowly realize that personal *boundaries are dissolving*. They find themselves doing and thinking things that surprise even themselves.

The loved one, for example, steals money from the family, something he'd never previously considered, or a wife cruises a sordid neighborhood looking for her husband, or perhaps borrows money from her brother to help pay off a drug debt. The dissolution of boundaries continues as long as the drug use continues, leading to behaviors that are perplexing, shameful, and risky. And crossing one boundary makes it that much easier to cross another.

Though it often seems otherwise, *denial* is not the same as lying. For a person in deep denial, the perception of the truth has been so dramatically impacted by needs and desires that the lie becomes the truth. Even though it's obvious to everyone that A causes B, the person in denial will say otherwise, thinking he's telling the truth. The near-acronym for "DENIAL" says it all: "Don't Even Know I Am Lying."

Because of the power of drugs, the addicted person's distortion of the truth is far greater than that experienced by normal people when confronted by normal desires. In time, with continued drug use and disease progression, this unremitting distortion produces a brain dysfunction wherein denial becomes a "state of being" for the addicted individual. His perception of himself and the world around him becomes blurred, tainted, and unreal.

This chemically induced denial process ensures that the addicted person will be unable to connect any troubling event to his drug use. It prevents him from seeing that the event is merely a normal occurrence that can be overcome by normal means. In this way the disease of addiction is self-perpetuating. After causing a problem, the drug then disguises itself as the cure for that problem. As aptly put by one recovering individual, "I kept using that which broke me, thinking it would fix me."

To hide his addiction and avoid confrontation, the addicted person often employs *triangulation*. Picture a triangle with the addicted person at the top. At each lower point you can place the people or institutions that find themselves in conflict over issues involving the addicted person's behavior.

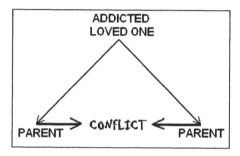

A common triangulation involves two parents battling each other over problems concerning their addicted child. Other combatants may include grand-parents, in-laws, the legal system, or even the addiction treatment program. Distraught, they blame each other for the mounting consequences in their loved one's life. Those individuals pitted against one another become distracted and lose sight of the real problem in their lives: the addiction. This has the effect of relieving the addicted person from responsibility for his behavior.

For families to successfully intervene in their loved one's addiction they must first cease fighting with each other and everyone else. They must remain separate from their loved one's legal battles, custody disputes, and employment disagreements. The addicted person wants someone else to enter into these conflicts so that he can avoid the stress of the consequences that were created by him in the first place. *When you help your loved one avoid a consequence you are guaranteeing that he will suffer a harsher consequence later.*

When drug use continues, *maturation cessation* sets in. Facing and dealing with the normal disappointments and failures in life add to healthy emotional development and learning. If drugs are used to "solve" these difficulties, emotional growth is stunted. Families then develop a distorted view of the true, chronological age of their addicted loved one. In their minds he's still a child and they treat him as such.

As feelings of anxiety and depression deepen, a *joylessness* permeates much of the addicted person's life. Previously pleasurable activities are now burdensome chores. A walk through a colorful forest is bleak and barren; family gatherings are dull; playing with the kids is a boring obligation.

While many people in the early stage of addiction continue to pursue their careers and maintain family relationships, those in the middle stage often do so because they think they should, not because they want to. The elements of life that previously provided happiness and motivation have now become tasks. And when the addicted person's life becomes filled with nothing but tasks he looks for greater pleasures. For him, alcohol and drugs are handy, rapid-acting rewards. Getting high becomes the focus of living.

At this stage the addicted person becomes increasingly *powerless* over his behavior. As they say in AA, it's "self-will run riot." The decision to use or not to use no longer exists. There are no more options. Unable to see the impact his behavior is having on others, the addicted person is engulfed by selfishness and self-centeredness. And although denial prevents him from realizing it, he's also burdened with guilt and shame.

> ➤ *Late Stage*

Symptoms of the late stage of addiction include:

- *physical adaptation*
- *decreasing tolerance*
- *cravings*
- *physical problems*
- *loss of interest*
- *isolation*
- *lessening of denial*
- *hopelessness*

Physiological Manifestations

Another way of describing addiction is *physical adaptation* to a drug. By the late stage, the body has adapted entirely to the presence of the substance and needs it to just barely function. Without the drug the body reacts with severe withdrawal symptoms. Depending on the drug involved, these can vary from the intense, flu-like symptoms of opiates, to the extreme agitation of cocaine and methamphetamine, or to the life-threatening delirium tremens produced by alcohol. Relief can only be obtained by taking more of the drug in the quantity the drug demands. The addicted person is no longer living to use; he's using to live.

Also during the late stage of addiction, the addicted individual will experience a *decreasing tolerance* for the drug. Since his body is no longer able to efficiently metabolize the substance, smaller amounts produce toxicity. Late stage alcoholics, for example, unable to continue their previous consumption, face a dilemma: their bodies demand the chemical but the toxic effects prevent them from ingesting enough to forestall the symptoms of withdrawal. These intolerable effects are experienced because the damaged liver, once functioning like a highly stoked furnace, is now choking on ethyl alcohol. Individuals addicted to opiates also experience decreasing tolerance and will frequently overdose. Life for the late stage addicted person is a living hell caused by a body that is incapable of satisfying its own demands.

By now the body is no longer subtle in its demand for the drug. Powerful *cravings* intensify which become unlike any desire ever experienced. The drug is now in complete command. It decides when and how much to use, when and what to eat, when to sleep, and when to socialize, if at all. With unequalled intensity, the cravings disrupt normal behavior and override any effort to say no.

Addiction causes an almost infinite array of associated *physical problems,* depending on the specific drug or drugs involved. The list includes high blood pressure, hepatitis, pancreatitis, gastrointestinal disorders, kidney disease, heart disease, and muscular disabilities. Because of the prevalence of comorbidities, it's essential that addicted individuals receive a thorough medical evaluation at the onset of addiction treatment.

Psychosocial Manifestations

In the late stage of addiction your loved one will *lose interest* in the normal events of life. He may actually desire to be a part of family activities but he'll rarely be able to participate. The effects of the drug itself notwithstanding, the underlying motivation has evaporated. Previously important activities just don't matter anymore.

One result of complete control by the drug and a loss of interest in most activities is *isolation* from family and previous friends. Some relationships might continue, but only with other addicted people. The rare contact that your loved one might have with family members is generally only an effort to obtain money or satisfy some other need.

During the early and especially the middle stages of his disease, your loved one was deep in denial. This not only prevented him from knowing that he had a problem but it also rejected any suggestions concerning recovery. In the late stage, however, the *denial may dissipate* and become supplanted by feelings of *hopelessness*. Your loved one can rapidly flip from "I don't have a problem" to "My problem is so bad that I can't be helped." This hopelessness plays right into the hands of the addiction. The diseased brain can now tell the addicted person that it's impossible to recover and that he might just as well go ahead and use.

Of course this hopelessness is unfounded. The recovery movement was originally started by people in the late stage of addiction and people today continue to recover from this so-called hopeless stage. But in recent years the number of people entering recovery from middle stage addiction has been on the upswing. Educational and treatment interventions are more effective now, and those who have recovered from late stage addiction share their motivating "stories," powerful messages that prove that addiction can and should be recognized and treated as early as possible.

The Resources section (Appendix D) at the end of this book provides a beginning for your addiction education. The HBO *Addiction* DVD includes interviews with family members, people in recovery, and experts in the field. The Internet, when used judiciously, is a powerful tool for accessing mountains of informative material. The Alcoholics Anonymous website at www.alcoholics-anonymous.org is a source for learning about that organization and locating meetings in your area. The DVD companion to this book, *Baffled by Addiction? A Seven Part Series for Loved Ones,* contains live Loved Ones Group discussions facilitated by Ed Hughes.

Chapter Highlights and Suggestions

- Understand that addiction is a chronic, progressive disease

- Your loved one experienced a greater than normal pleasurable response from alcohol and drugs

- In effect, your loved one experienced a side effect of the drug

- Addiction is not due to weak moral character, stress or traumatic events, weak will-power, an addictive personality, high-risk environment, or low self-esteem

- Early recognition of the disease increases the chance for earlier recovery

- Addiction progresses through identifiable stages with characteristic physiological and psychosocial manifestations

- The family begins rescuing the loved one from the problems introduced in the middle stage of addiction

- Expand your knowledge of addiction by using all available resources

2) Don't Rescue

It's extremely rare for anyone to be "loved" into recovery. People with addictions must be allowed to accumulate sufficient negative consequences related to their drinking or drug use to obtain the necessary motivation to initiate a recovery effort. They must first hit a personal bottom.

Sometimes not doing something can be more painful than taking action, and this is certainly true of not rescuing. To sit back and watch your loved one suffer the consequences of his disease can bring you to your emotional knees. During this mutual suffering it's difficult to visualize that any sort of progress is being made. In fact, it seems as though everything is moving backwards and getting worse.

The challenge is to maintain a perspective that includes the entire process, to keep telling yourself that *only by allowing your loved one to experience the consequences of his disease will he reach the point where he will make a decision to accept help.* It's also essential to keep in mind that the sooner this happens the better because rescuing comes with a promise: it guarantees that your loved one will face another, more serious, consequence. And it might be one that you're not able to fix.

Truth...

Denial does a cunning job of hiding the truth of addiction. Denial is so effective, in fact, that the truth remains hidden from both the addicted loved one and his family. But if family members are to be helpful in any way at all, they must first discover and accept the truth. Progress cannot begin until the loved one's disease is openly and frankly admitted. It makes no difference that the truth may originate from an outside source, such as a friend, television commercial, or judge. Sooner or later the reality must be shared. The truth of the matter is a matter of truth.

The addicted person's initial response to hearing the truth will almost always be negative. His reaction might be angry, defensive, or accusatory: "How dare you!" or "No way I'm addicted!" or "The cops are to blame!" The exact form will vary but will nearly always be one of rejection.

Look for an opportunity to state the truth, but don't force it. A chance may arise in an otherwise normal situation, such as when you're asked for the keys to the family car. Simply indicate the obvious and avoid an argument. "You use drugs so you can't have the car." You've no need to defend the truth. And rest assured that once the truth is spoken, it will not be forgotten. Recovering people have referred to this as "the haunting." Those words of truth, once uttered, will be imbedded in your loved one's mind forever.

...and Consequences

But because your loved one's mind is being held hostage by his disease, the truth alone will not lead to a change. He must also be allowed to experience consequences.

Don't pretend that there is no problem and that everything is normal. Excuses can be made for every crisis and blame assigned to everything but the addiction. "Oh, that's just Johnny" or "He's just going through a phase" or "His boss doesn't understand him." Each time a problem is fixed—by providing money, paying the fine, or hiring a lawyer—the consequences are removed which, in turn, guarantees the occurrence of another crisis. If he's in a jam, let him stay there. The consequences just might get him into recovery sooner than you thought possible. Saying "no" is often the most loving thing a person can do.

As the disease progresses and the addicted person gets sicker, the experienced consequences—the crises—increase in both intensity and frequency. Removing the consequences is rescuing and only assures the occurrence of another crisis of greater magnitude. One possible course is to allow the crises to continue to intensify until the rescuers—the family members—are *unable* to remove the consequence. "I tried, but I couldn't keep him out of prison." But a better course—and this is the key—is for the family to become *unwilling* to rescue. Only when the addicted person feels the full impact of his behavior—by experiencing consequences—will the crises cease.

What follows is an age-related timeline that couples an addicted person's abnormal activities with his family's rescuing responses. Note especially that the magnitude of the aberrant behavior increases with time.

Age	Activity	Response/Result
15	Stayed out too late	Grounded, but rarely enforced
16	Changed friends	Complained about new friends
17	Drank while underage	Scolded about drinking

18	Flunked out of college	Lost tuition money
18	Asked to move home	Allowed to move back home
18	Unemployed	Encouraged but did not insist on employment
18	Continued drinking	Confronted about drinking
19	Began drug use	Gave money for "gas and groceries"
20	Smoked pot at home	Accepted story that pot belonged to someone else
23	Asked to start a business	Supported the business financially
23	Moved in with girlfriend	Provided rent
23	Received DUI	Paid for bail, attorney, drivers' license reinstatement; said would never bail out again
24	Only part time at business	Gave money to pay bills
25	Conflict with girlfriend over drug use	Asked girlfriend not to move out
26	Bought Rx painkillers off street	Kept suspicions a secret
28	Borrowed from other family members	Said nothing to other family members
28	Received second DUI, charged with Rx drug possession	Bailed out, paid for attorney, paid for mandated treatment
29	Moved back home	Allowed to move back home
29	Moved back with girlfriend, had child	Paid rent, helped support child
30	Business struggled	Supported business financially
30	Moved back home, fell behind on child support	Allowed to move back home; paid child support
31	Re-arrested for drug possession; plea-bargained for five years probation	Paid for attorney, legal fees
31	Probation violation (positive drug screen)	Paid for attorney, legal fees

32	Sentenced to three years in prison	Unable to help

At any point along this timeline, a non-rescuing interruption could have prevented the next consequence. Said another way, an early omission in the right-hand column could have led to a higher bottom in the left-hand column. The result would have been earlier entry into treatment.

Rescuing

A character in a movie once said wistfully, "I'd worry a whole lot less if you'd worry a whole lot more." Worry should be a natural consequence for someone not taking care of business or engaging in high-risk behaviors. Rescuing, which often begins with prompting or reminding the addicted person of his daily tasks and obligations, effectively relieves the addicted person of all his worries. The more the rescuer worries, the less the addicted person worries and a consequence—worry—is thereby removed. Although this "caretaking" behavior is meant to prevent and remove undesirable events from occurring, it's actually a powerful type of rescuing which assures that additional, more serious consequences will be encountered.

Ironically, the doting family member often becomes the target of the addicted person's anger. Even though he depends on this family member's prompting, he simultaneously deeply resents the dependency and the associated loss of self-esteem.

Also, because people are basically capable of running only one life (their own), as the addicted person's disease progresses it becomes increasingly stressful to manage his life as well. As the rescuer responds by giving more time and attention to the addicted person, other family members become jealous and resentful when their needs are left unmet.

You may find that you or other family members have been guilty of other forms of rescuing your loved one, such as:

- Providing a "shoulder to cry on"
- Participating in the "blame game"—blaming something else for his problems
- Taking care of his kids
- Protecting him from legal consequences
- Providing employment in the family business
- Providing transportation
- Providing meals
- Keeping secrets
- Not telling other family members about his disease
- Treating him like a child
- Worrying about the consequences instead of the disease
- Making excuses for him
- Extracting promises
- Pretending that everything is normal
- Lowering your expectations
- Accepting a relationship with increasing limitations
- Allowing yourself to be in a parenting "role" rather than an adult "relationship"
- Allowing yourself to be the target of anger, threats, or violence

The following conversation took place following a Loved Ones session:

Father: My son has hit rock bottom.

Ed: Tell me about that.

Father: Well, he's in jail after his third DUI. He's facing lots of problems.

Ed: Let's talk about just the last thing that happened. He got picked up for his third DUI?

Father: That's right.

Ed: What happened then?

Father: Well, I went and got him out of jail.

Ed: How'd you do that?

Father: I had to put up a $500 bond.

Ed: Then what happened?

Father: Well, he lost his driver's license too.

Ed: How's he getting around?

Father: His mother and I are driving him around. He can't work anymore; he lost his job.

Ed: So how is he paying his bills?

Father: Well, we're paying his bills. We're keeping things going. We're keeping up his apartment, giving him grocery money, that kind of thing.

Ed: Somebody hit rock bottom, all right, but I don't think it was your son.

Some stories demonstrate the power of denial as it affects both the addicted person and the family:

> I was sitting in jail after getting my third DUI and a possession charge. I was miserable. My dad had promised he would never bail me out again, but I called him anyway. On the phone he said he wasn't coming to get me. As I sat in that jail I looked around and thought how my life had become such a mess because of my use of drugs and alcohol, how I had disappointed myself and everyone around me. How I had lost my girlfriend whom I love and loved me, loved me so much she couldn't stand to see me kill myself. I looked around at the other inmates and for the first time I saw myself exactly like them, no different. I had to do something, I had to get help.
>
> At that moment the jailer came to the cell and told me that my father was there to take me home. I was elated and my first thought was I'm glad I'm not like the other people in here. All the previous thoughts of getting help left my mind immediately and all I could think about was that I needed a drink and what would I have to put up with from my dad. He was going to blame me and it wasn't my fault. The cops had no right to stop me, I wasn't drunk, and the

cocaine they found in my car was left
there by a friend earlier in the evening.

This family finally stopped rescuing. The son soon
had another incident, experienced the consequences of
his disease, and made a decision to get help.

While saying "no" and sticking with your response
can be extremely difficult, on the positive side saying
"no" gets easier with time. Each encounter dealt with
successfully makes the next challenge less onerous.
Because addiction is desperate to receive your cooperation and hates not getting what it wants, your
loved one will make numerous efforts to get you to
change your mind. If you do succumb, he will be that
much more determined and persistent next time.
Expect him to use a variety of manipulative responses,
including anger, pleading, guilt-production, threats,
and baiting.

> I basically raised my grandson. I tried to
> give him the things he needed and
> wanted. He was a good boy until he got
> involved with drugs. For a long time I
> didn't know what was going on. Even
> when I finally admitted to myself what
> the problem was, I still couldn't say "no"
> to him; I couldn't stop trying to fix what-
> ever problems he got himself into. As he
> got more out of control, he got more in
> control of me. It got to the point where
> he totally dominated my life. I'd give
> him money, leave work to give him
> rides, and get numerous phone calls
> from him every day.

The first time I said "no" was to a small request he made over the phone. The reaction I got made it seem like I'd denied him air to breathe. First he was furious, then he pleaded and called me names, and then he said I didn't love him. He told me that terrible things would happen to him if I didn't give him what he wanted. It was awful. Because it was a phone call, I was able to keep saying "no" but after I hung up he called back several times. I tried to reason with him but I finally had to turn the phone off.

This was a turning point for me: saying "no" to a minor request. Within a couple of months my relationship with my grandson changed dramatically. I began to detach both from his sickness and the demands the sickness was placing on me. Eventually I decided that he should leave my home. That decision was terribly difficult but was actually much easier than the first time I ever said "no."

Our relationship was severely limited for several months but one day he called and asked me to help him. He wanted to come home and get help for his addiction. By now I'd been coached on how to handle a request like this so I gave my grandson the phone number of the treatment agency that had helped me with my rescuing behavior.

He's currently in extended treatment. The plan is for him not to return to my home because neither of us can trust ourselves not to get caught up in our old behavior. Today we're working on a new relationship and it's tough. It's better than what we had, though, and for the first time in years I have hope that we can get through this and be better because of it.

Family Roles

The family's initial response to the early crises of addiction is role-playing, and the central character in this melodrama is the primary rescuer. All other roles are secondary and exist only in response to the activities of this lead player.

➢ Primary Rescuer

The primary rescuer is like the point guard on a basketball team or an executive secretary in a busy corporation. The addicted individual will turn to this key person when trouble comes and expect him to deliver. This person orchestrates events either to prevent problems from occurring or to extract the addicted person from trouble after the fact. The primary rescuer deals with apologies and promises, two of the addicted individual's crisis tools: "I'm sorry about that. It'll never happen again." Extracting a promise is not only an attempt to establish an adult relationship with the addicted person but also serves to reward the rescuer for his rescuing. This effort, however, only ensures that yet another crisis will occur because your loved one's addiction makes it impossible for him to keep a promise.

This primary rescuer is pivotal to the addicted person's ability to avoid the consequences of his behavior. While attempting to enroll other family members, this person plans strategies that anticipate and eliminate crises. Because the addicted person will go first to the primary rescuer for help, money, or sympathy, this is the most stressful role of all. This person is the safety net for the addicted loved one.

➤ *Secondary Roles*

Another family member may assume the role of critic. This person, though secretly grateful for the actions of the primary rescuer, steps aside and scrutinizes from a distance. The criticism, which often entails suggestions to stop rescuing, only motivates the primary rescuer to rescue even more. However, should the primary rescuer become unable or unwilling to rescue further, the critic steps in as a secondary rescuer, becomes the addicted person's back-up, and resumes the rescuing. A balancing act between the primary rescuer and the critic thus emerges. If the critic should then remove himself from the situation, the primary rescuer regains the equilibrium by rescuing even more fervently.

Grandparents are in a special category because they often find themselves in an impossible situation. Not only do they witness the suffering of their addicted adult child, but they often must also experience the parental neglect of their grandchildren. Nothing produces a level of worry as intense as realizing that one's grandchildren are at risk or lacking basic needs. Here the policy of "not rescuing" can still be practiced, but with limitations that recognize the involvement of the grandchildren. In this scenario, the following recommendations can be helpful:

- If you must help, give your help directly to the grandchildren; never give money directly to your addicted child; if a parent asks for money for diapers, buy the diapers yourself

- Don't hesitate to involve legal or child welfare authorities

- If you are already providing a significant amount of care for the grandchildren, consider seeking custody

- If they are old enough, talk to the grandchildren about the problem in their home and encourage them to contact you if:
  o they feel they are in danger,
  o they are left alone, or
  o their parents are unable to care for them

- Keep in mind that if the parents don't experience their conse-

- quences, the problems will escalate and the risks to the grandchildren will intensify

Siblings involved in the addiction melodrama assume a variety of roles. The fretter is consumed with worry about her loved one but has no resources to provide help in times of crisis. Emotionally tortured by the addicted person's struggles, the fretter has no power to fix anything.

Another child may have serious life problems that go unnoticed because of the attention focused on the addicted loved one. The problem may be an emerging addiction or other health or emotional difficulty that does not create a level of crisis sufficient to distract attention from the family's focus.

Other children in the family are just forgotten. Lost in the swirl of activity that centers on the addicted loved one, they become angry and resentful. They finally grow weary of seeing so much attention and family resources spent on someone so undeserving.

Boundaries

As mentioned earlier, the addicted individual sets boundaries for himself from the very start of his drug use. With every good intention he tries to control his use and behavior. "I'll only use on weekends." And then he's using every day. "I'll never steal." And next he's into his mother's purse. The powerlessness created by his addiction means that he'll cross every boundary and then set new ones, which will be violated as well. His craving brain rationalizes the need for new boundaries.

Families also set boundaries but they become erased by rescuing. "We're never getting you out of jail again!" And next week they're putting up bail. "You can't use the car any more!" And then the car keys are turned over once again. The line in the sand is wiped out and a new one is drawn. Just like the addicted person's disease, the rescuing process is progressive.

Family members find themselves assuming responsibility for the addicted person's obligations. They may begin by paying his rent or providing room and board and then progress to taking care of other financial responsibilities, such as taking care of legal fines or providing money for the needs of the grandchildren. So many boundaries are crossed that no boundaries remain. The separateness disappears. And while this "boundarylessness" continues, the family is likely berating, cajoling, and doing everything they can think of to get the addicted loved one to take responsibility.

A mother described her life as "boundaryless" and told of her relationship with her forty-year-old son:

> Each morning I call him at his home to wake him up for work. If he can't go to work I call his employer and tell them he's sick. I fix his breakfast and take it to him. I gather his clothes and clean his house. I get his money so I can pay his bills, and I give him an allowance. I've been trying to help him get his drivers' license back, which he lost

because of DUIs. He's got a teenage
daughter who lives with her mother. I
buy her presents and birthday cards and
send them on his behalf.

This true story, though extreme, is an example of
"late stage" rescuing. This mother had crossed so
many boundaries that there were no more to cross.

Identifying Your Role

Since roles develop in response to a loved one's
addiction, it's important that family members identify
their specific reactions to both crises and regular, day-
to-day problems. Such responses may include:

- making excuses for the loved one's behavior
- providing regular financial support, such as
  rent or spending money
- providing crisis financial support, such as after
  an arrest or loss of employment
- providing a "shoulder to cry on" in response to
  consequences created by addiction
- advocating for the addicted person in conflicts
  with family members, employers, or the legal
  system
- keeping secrets on behalf of the loved one,
  especially from other family members
- attempting to talk the loved one into getting
  help or acting properly
- serving as the loved one's brain by reminding
  him of daily responsibilities, such as keeping

appointments, paying bills, and making
probation visits
- providing housing and other basic living needs
- worrying about the consequences that the loved
one is suffering
- actively working to solve the loved one's daily
difficulties
- criticizing the primary rescuer, which only
serves to further solidify that role

These examples of common activities that rescue
addicted loved ones from their consequences can
allow each family member the necessary task of assessing his behavior when faced with the effects of addiction. This provides the basis for identifying those
behaviors that *need to be changed.* This difficult process, which is of the utmost importance and value,
becomes the beginning of disentanglement from the
mess of addiction.

To further evaluate your role ask yourself:

- "Do I get angry or feel sorry for my
loved one?"
- "Do I extract promises as barter for my
agreement to provide help?"
- "Do I provide money?"
- "Do I become an active participant in
his plan to escape the consequences?"
- "How am I manipulated?"
- "How do I respond to the melodrama
of addiction?"
- "What conflicts do I incur by rescuing
my loved one?"

- "What actions do I take on a daily basis to help my loved one?"

As you answer these questions and the more general "What am I doing to prevent my loved one from experiencing his consequences?" question, you'll begin to develop a list of behaviors that need to be changed in order to become disentangled from your loved one and begin the process of healing yourself.

$$+ + +$$

Chapter Highlights and Suggestions

- Denial effectively conceals the truth of addiction

- The consequences caused by the addiction increase in both magnitude and frequency

- Rescuing guarantees that another, greater crisis will occur

- Family members assume "roles" as the "relationship" with their loved one evaporates

- Both family members and their loved one create boundaries that are eventually violated

- Refraining from rescuing enhances the chances of your loved one recovering from his addiction

- Identify your role in response to crises and normal daily difficulties

- Saying "no" to rescuing is one of the most difficult—and loving—things you can do for your loved one

3) Don't Support the Addiction Financially

Giving money to your loved one is another form of rescuing and, due to its pervasiveness and impact on the disease of addiction, deserves special attention. Families often see money as a quick and easy solution to many of the problems created by addiction. Indeed, money will quiet the waters for a while, but only until the next crisis, which will require more money.

Addiction Depends on Money

Rest assured that most of the money that you give your loved one will find its way to the liquor store or drug dealer. Even small amounts of money can be enough to get him through another day of addiction. His expressed need might be groceries, car repairs, or court fines, but cash received for those expenses will be used properly only after the addiction is satisfied.

Money is the lifeblood of addiction. Stop the money and you create an opportunity for your loved one to get well. He'll be faced with the consequences of his disease, an experience necessary for recovery. The absence of money—a true consequence—can be your loved one's personal bottom leading to treatment.

It's also important to realize that if giving money to your loved one has been part of your role, money was probably a central reason for his continued involvement with you. If you stop giving money, you may find that you'll have only limited contact with your loved one. This difficult commitment, however, will have the desired effect of allowing him to experience the consequences of his disease.

Looking at actual costs, alcohol is cheap but alcoho*lism* is expensive. True costs must consider all the related "family" expenses such as DUIs, car repairs, legal fees, high-risk automobile insurance, living at home, bad financial decisions, and divorce.

A recovering fellow reached into his wallet and brought out his driver's license. "I have over $6,000 invested in this card," he said with a grin. He was referring, of course, to the legal fees, court costs, reinstatement fees, car repairs, and high-risk insurance associated with impaired driving.

Drugs, on the other hand, are expensive and can, by themselves, bankrupt you. In addition to the other "family" expenses, which might include lawyers' fees after a theft, bad checks or credit card debt, a $100-plus per day habit can be financially devastating. At this writing, Oxycontin was selling on the street for a dollar a milligram; the average daily usage was two 80-milligram tablets, or 160 milligrams.

One mother shared the financial burden she experienced as a result of her adult daughter's drug addiction:

- her daughter's rent
- child care for two grandchildren
- two automobiles lost in accidents
- attorney and court fees to avoid jail time
- $50 per week cash for gas, groceries, and "miscellaneous" items
- $2,000 to repay family members for money stolen by her daughter

- hospital detoxification bills
- debt from a credit card stolen by her daughter (used for cash advances for drugs)

Not surprisingly, this mother was left struggling with her own finances and damaged credit.

This story is not unusual and is not isolated to families with abundant resources. Addiction will take and take and take some more until the money runs out. The harsh reality is that most of the money acquired by the addicted person will end up in the pocket of the drug dealer. Any that remains is used to pay for some consequence caused by the addiction.

A young man in recovery told this story:

> I knew I was in big trouble with my family when I came home to find my parents and wife sitting around the kitchen table waiting for me. My wife had called and told them about my drug use and that we didn't have enough money to pay our bills because I had spent my paycheck on drugs. My father was furious and my wife and mother were crying. My first inclination was to turn around and head for the door, but I needed money to pay the bills, plus I needed some drug money. So I sat down and let my father yell at me. I listened to my mom talk about how disappointed she was, and my wife talk about how afraid she was that we were

going to lose everything. We talked half the night. I cried and promised I would do better. I even got a chance to tell the three of them where I thought they were at fault. It was very emotional. At the end we all hugged and said how much we loved each other. My parents left but not before leaving an envelope of money for us to use to pay our bills. My wife went to bed and I called a friend and told him to bring me the drugs. I paid for them with part of the money my parents had left for our bills.

Don't Manage the Money

Because addicted people are financially irresponsible, family members will often try to help by assuming control of their funds. This doesn't work. Keep in mind that your goal is to disentangle yourself from your loved one's addiction and the consequences it creates. A consequence of the disease is the inability to manage finances properly and this must be experienced by your loved one.

While people with addiction problems rarely reach their employment potential, the majority are employed, at least during the early and middle stages of their disease. But as the drug progressively impacts their brains and impairs judgment, they make increasingly poor financial decisions. As a result, and because of the large sums spent on drugs, they rely more and more on the resources of others to support their daily needs.

Families are hesitant to withdraw support, believing that everything will "fall apart" if they cease helping. Ironically, "falling apart" is what should be allowed happen. Your loved one will not get better if he's continually propped up by your financial support or management. And there is little else that will disrupt your relationship with him more than your efforts to control his finances. An addicted person's financial life is a mess and will become progressively worse. You need to stay as far away from the mess as possible.

Also beware that you can provide ill-advised financial support in ways other than direct cash contributions. Paying for rent, food, and car repairs are all forms of financial support. Anytime you pay for something that is properly the responsibility of the addicted person, you free up his money to buy drugs, spend irresponsibly, and avoid a consequence of his disease.

+ + +

Chapter Highlights and Suggestions

- Addiction depends on money

- Providing financial support of any kind during active addiction is rescuing

- You will see less of your loved one once you stop giving him money

- Alcohol is cheap but drugs are expensive

- Managing your loved one's finances won't work

4) Don't Analyze the Drug Use

The only answer to the "why" question is because your loved one took a drink or drug and became addicted. The stress, depression, and anger are the results—not the causes—of his disease. The family is never the cause of the addiction. If you do ask "why," the blame will only end up back on you. The addicted person desperately wants to project the responsibility for the disease onto other people and other things. That's the essence of alcologic.

Have you ever had one of those lengthy, heart-to-heart conversations with your loved one either during or following a crisis? The discussion, perhaps lasting well into the night, likely contained some truth and everyone accepted some blame. In the end everyone cried and hugged. (If this occurred immediately after a crisis that had been fixed by the family, your loved one was probably very cooperative and agreeable.) Afterward the family members, feeling much better, were left with new hope that things were going to change.

But did anything change? No. In the eyes of your loved one, these heart-to-hearts are merely annoying inconveniences. They represent the price he has to pay for being rescued. Efforts to "figure out" what is causing the drug use are futile and a waste of time. The analyzing eventually results in pain and disappointment; the change that seemed on the verge of occurring either never happens or is short-lived.

As the disease progresses, the addicted person maintains a continuously evolving "story." Over time the story becomes complex, but generally serves to explain the drug use and abnormal behavior and to distract from the addiction itself. The shared elements that run through every addicted person's story include some or all of the following:

Blaming

From the beginning addicted people struggle to avoid taking responsibility for their actions. It's the nature of addiction to remove the blame from the person's drug use and place it somewhere else, such as with a family member, employer, or bad luck. The story of blame is a distraction to draw the family's attention to another issue. "It's my depression, not the drug use, that's the problem." The distraction can also take the form of a threat: "I'm leaving town" or "I'm going to kill myself."

Because it's difficult to admit that a loved one is addicted and also responsible for the behaviors that follow, family members often make things worse by joining the blame game. This fuels the loved one's story with even more accusations. And when family members begin blaming each other, the game becomes particularly painful and destructive.

The family is exceedingly vulnerable to assuming responsibility for the presence of the addiction. "Where did I go wrong?" is a question asked repeatedly. Without a doubt a connection exists between the addicted person's skill at blaming others and the family's willingness to accept the blame. Even the children of an addicted parent often feel somehow responsible. Because guilt causes family members to cross their own boundaries and resort once more to rescuing behavior, they must challenge their own conceptions of their role in the disease. Remember: you are dealing with a disease caused by no one.

Rationalizing

The addicted individual always has a "reason" or "excuse" for whatever happens or goes wrong. This effort to make the irrational seem rational is another example of alcologic: upside down thinking. The addicted person is constantly rationalizing to himself; for every excuse you hear, he has told himself dozens more. His rational mind, which is trying to point out the irrationality of his behavior, eventually becomes overwhelmed by the powerful influence of the drug. Then, with the onset of denial, he's unable to determine the truth.

Isolating

Another form of defense used by the addicted person is hiding. At first it's an attempt to conceal the drug use, but eventually he'll avoid people who might either disapprove of his behavior or offer help. Isolation is an indication of disease progression; your loved one will eventually disassociate from family and social gatherings that are not a part of his drinking or drugging subculture.

Minimizing

"It's not that bad" is a common refrain used by the addicted person. In his world he's constantly comparing himself to others struggling with their ad-dictions. "If I ever get as bad as him I'll quit." Then, when your loved one does get as bad, he'll find some-one else for comparison. The addicted individual is continually drawing lines in the sand, erasing them, and drawing new ones. "I would never use crack cocaine" is followed by snorting. "I would never use a needle" is followed by intravenous injections. As the addiction takes control of the brain, it also assumes control of the mind. The addicted brain-mind works like a bodyguard to prevent the addicted individual from seeing the truth.

Manipulating

Your loved one knows what scares you. He'll use this knowledge of your vulnerabilities to manipulate you into rescuing him, giving in to his demands, or abandoning your threats. The bomb he drops may be, "You don't love me!" or "I'll leave with the kids and you'll never see them again!" In most instances your response should be to entirely ignore the comments, but there is an important exception:

Threatening Suicide

In the event that your loved one threatens physical harm to himself or someone else, you should contact the proper authority which, in most cases, is law en-forcement. Don't attempt to negotiate, plead, or inter-vene. If your loved one is in fact suicidal, he needs immediate professional help, something the family is not equipped to provide. If, on the other hand, the threat is emotional manipulation, and if you contact the authorities, you probably won't be bothered by that antic again. Either way, your ability to withstand the "bomb threat" and not get caught up in the melodrama becomes a valuable turning point in the role-relationship with your loved one.

Many addicted people thrive on melodrama. As a result of excessive self-centeredness caused by the addiction, they envision themselves at the center of the universe, an unfortunate viewpoint often shared by the worried family. In a scene from *Beaches,* Bette Midler, while rambling on about her accomplishments in life, pauses to suggest to her longtime friend, "OK, enough of me talking about me. Now you talk about me." Addicted people become addicted to the crises that have become their lives.

And too often family members become addicted to this crisis-oriented lifestyle as well. They seem to jump at the chance to go off posse-like into the night on a journey of rescue or catastrophe prevention. Then, when the disaster is resolved and the tension abates, the addicted person expresses neither interest nor appreciation. A crisis, then, is no longer a crisis for the addicted person as soon as someone else begins to fix it.

The symptoms of blaming, rationalizing, isolating, minimizing, and manipulating demonstrate that addiction has many faces and that no amount of scrutiny will cause your loved one to enter treatment. This "paralysis by analysis" only distracts from your commitment to not rescue.

As the disease progresses family members feel trapped. Every thought of action is followed by another thought of what the consequences will be if they don't help or rescue. Family members frequently seek a "painless" solution, living each day hoping that something miraculous will happen and their loved one will change. Something miraculous *can* happen but usually will not if the family is standing in the way of the very consequences that will provide the motivation for the start of recovery.

Chapter Highlights and Suggestions

- Efforts to determine the cause of your loved one's addiction are a waste of time

- The family is never to blame

- Don't join the blame game

- Your loved one uses alcologic: upside down thinking

- Expect your loved one to rationalize, isolate, minimize, and manipulate

- If suicide is threatened, call the authorities

5) Don't Make Idle Threats, Preach, or Lecture

Words Don't Work

The least effective tool when dealing with an addicted person is words. No matter how convincing you may sound, your loved one will ordinarily just shut down and wait you out. Sometimes he may openly object to your lecture, but more often he'll be patient, knowing that he'll finally get what he wants anyway. The urge to lecture derives from your own frustrations, fears, and desires to help. In fact it merely prolongs the pretense that new knowledge will bring about a change in your loved one. Even sharing the material presented in this book will be ineffective; he'll remain deaf to all forms of verbal logic.

Nor does threatening help. Your loved one doesn't believe you because you've never followed through before. Threats coming from credible, non-family sources, however, can be effective. A judge promising prison or an employer threatening dismissal holds water if the addicted person believes that a consequence will actually ensue. A probation officer will not lose any sleep if your loved one experiences a threatened consequence. In these situations the family should not interfere, for therein may lie the key that motivates your loved one toward recovery.

So following through with your intentions is paramount. Your loved one must actually experience the consequence if it's to have any effect. "Reality is when it happens to me."

Another futile effort is to persist in parenting your loved one after he has reached adulthood. This frequently occurs if your loved one continues to live at home and remains dependent. The recurrent struggles to get him to clean up his room, take out the trash, and get a job only lead to frustration, anger, and discouragement. But more importantly, these failed attempts at parenting completely avoid addressing your loved one's addiction.

This well-intentioned mother finally gave in:

> I was driving home from work and my mind was busy with the conversation I was about to have with my adult daughter. I'd start off by telling her how much I loved her and that I only wanted what was best for her. Then I'd point out how her behavior was causing worry and problems for everyone. Her neglect of the family, her refusal to help out around the house, and her continual need for money was making life impossible.
>
> I'd been reading some information about addiction so I was going to educate her about the signs of addiction and tell her how she was displaying most of them. Then I was going to ask her to please get help—for the sake of everyone.
>
> When I got home I found her in front of the TV talking on her cell phone. I asked if I could talk with her but she just waved me off and kept on talking.

When she finally finished she started rushing around, changing her clothes, and telling me she needed to borrow my car. When I asked her where she was going and when she'd be back, she accused me of being nosey and reminded me that she was an adult. She also asked for $20. I told her I wanted to talk with her and started in on my prepared speech. Immediately after I said, "I love you and I want what's best for you," she exploded.

She said she was tired of me judging her and berating her and treating her like a kid. I said, "Well, you're acting like a kid. You don't work, you depend on our money, and you don't help around the house." As I spoke she got more agitated and angry. She told me what an awful mother I was and that all I cared about was money.

And then *I* got angry. I called her a spoiled brat drug addict. She started crying and I felt terrible. I apologized. I comforted her for a minute but then she said she had to leave. I gave her $20 as she walked out the door with my car keys.

Surprise Your Loved One

One effective approach is the surprise. Since your loved one depends on the predictability of rescuing for survival, a real consequence is when the consequence actually occurs. It's a shock when he comes around asking for money as usual but this time confronts a refusal. "No, I won't make your car payment." Simply state the truth without embellishment. "Your problems are due to your drug use." Don't add anything about counseling or treatment. "I can't let you have the keys to the car. You have a drug problem. That wouldn't make sense."

Family members only become frustrated when they attempt to change their loved one with words. Though they may spend hours agonizing over ways to "get through" and "convince" their loved one, the repeated failures will only serve to intensify their anger and frustration.

Chapter Highlights and Suggestions

- Words don't work

- Threats without follow-up actions do not help

- Surprise your loved one by allowing a consequence to occur

6) Don't Extract Promises

In the early stages of his addiction, the addicted individual retains a limited ability to say no to his disease. He's able, on most occasions, to confine his use to appropriate times and situations. As the disease progresses, however, so does his powerlessness; his capacity to say no is overwhelmed by his growing craving for the drug. The drug begins making the decisions. The addicted individual can keep a promise only if the drug doesn't demand otherwise.

This father learned about extracting promises the hard way:

> My son had been living on his own for two years. He'd gone to college for a couple of semesters but dropped out. He'd been doing a lot of drinking since high school and after his short stint in college he got addicted to prescription painkillers that he purchased from a drug dealer. Over time he sold everything he had, stole money or property from us, and had minor run-ins with the law.
>
> One day he called me (he always called me; his mother never gave him money) and said that he was in big trouble, that there'd been a big misunderstanding. His friend's family was accusing him of stealing some checks and forging the family's name on them.

The total was over $3,000. He told me he didn't steal the checks, that his friend had stolen them and was blaming it on him. He swore he was innocent.

Even though my wife said I was crazy to believe him, I thought he was telling me the truth this time. So I hired an attorney. My son turned himself in and I paid his bail. I made him promise to get help for his drug problem and he agreed.

The local treatment agency recommended that he be placed in a residential program but he opted for a short-term outpatient program, saying that he planned to get a job. He started attending his counseling sessions and moved back home (which his mother opposed) but I suspected he was still using drugs.

At the first court hearing the attorney came to me and presented the prosecutor's evidence. It was clear that my son had stolen the checks and committed forgery. The attorney said my son would probably go to prison if restitution to the family was not made. Needless to say I paid the money but not before making him promise to go into the residential program that the treatment agency had recommended in the first place. Reluctantly he agreed.

After the court case was dismissed, I met with my son to discuss his future. I agreed to pay for his residential treatment and help him find a job when he got out. He could live with us (again against my wife's wishes) until he got his feet on the ground. Then he could resume college and make something out of his life. He agreed, seemed interested, and promised to straighten out his life. Two weeks later he walked out of the treatment center.

After a disheartening period of experiencing their loved one's broken promises, family members lower their expectations. But not holding the loved one accountable amounts to rescuing. Family members must remember that getting angry, yelling, and berating are self-defeating. Not only are these futile behaviors not consequences, they actually have the opposite effect. The addicted person will dismiss your words—as he does all of your words—as being mean-spirited or just plain wrong.

Consider for a moment why you keep your own promises. It's out of self-respect, a sense of right and wrong, a desire to meet the expectations of others, or a concern for your reputation. For someone with a progressed addiction, however, these issues lost their influence long ago.

Despite appearances most addicted individuals deeply regret their trail of broken promises and feel guilty when they disappoint others. Though they have every intention of keeping their promises they're unable to do so. They don't yet understand the powerlessness created by their drug use. When asked, "Why didn't you keep your promise?" they have no answer.

When family members begin to understand their loved one's inability to keep promises, they need to ask themselves, "Why are we extracting promises?" Most often they are in the process of rescuing and want to justify their actions by extracting a promise, even knowing that the promise will not be kept. The promise makes them feel better about themselves. Then, when the next promise is broken, the family gets angry all over again, reprimands the loved one, and starts a new round of negotiations...until the next crisis.

The disease of addiction makes this promise: the addicted person can't keep promises. The addicted individual is unaware that he has a disease that renders him powerless. Later on he'll make promises that he *knows* he can't keep, as long as he believes he'll be rescued.

Traditional Interventions

In the context of addiction, *intervention* refers to a supposed interruption of the disease by a process involving a group of formally prepared, concerned individuals designed to encourage the addicted person to seek treatment. Participants may include addiction professionals, family members, close friends, clergy, or coworkers. Specific recommendations may consist of immediate residential or inpatient admission, early participation in intensive outpatient treatment, or prompt evaluation by a trained counselor.

The intervention model that was used for years proposed that family members, usually guided by an addiction professional, intervene with their loved one much like an organized ambush. They would confront him with guilt-producing tales of how he had harmed the family with the ultimate goal of getting him to agree to enter treatment.

While a number of people are sober today as a result of such an intervention, this method resembles a "fast food" approach to the recovery process. Too often the issues of rescuing and unhealthy relationships are never addressed. And later, when the addicted person exits treatment, he re-enters a family that is ill-prepared to face these other, unresolved elements of his addiction. This short-term technique overemphasizes the effectiveness of treatment and underestimates the power of the family to promote recovery.

Family Process Interventions

More appropriate is the *family process intervention,* whereby the family focuses on changing its role relative to the loved one, abandoning rescuing behavior, and shifting the consequences from the family to the addicted person. This process, though not quick or easy, has a number of advantages and benefits:

1. It helps to prepare your loved one for eventual treatment and recovery. While the importance of entering treatment as early as possible in the progression of the disease cannot be overemphasized, many individuals begin treatment before they are ready to quit drinking or using. If the addicted person is not experiencing the consequences of his disease, it's unlikely that he'll benefit substantially from any treatment that results from coercion. Families should do their work first—stop rescuing—and allow their loved one to experience his consequences. The addicted person will then be ready to accept the help offered by treatment professionals.

2. It prepares families for the long haul. A sad reality of addiction, which family members must accept, is that relapse occurs seventy percent of the time after the first entry into treatment and that it typically takes three or four attempts before finally succeeding. Since multiple episodes are the norm, families must prepare themselves for an extended process. This includes disentanglement from the drama, consequences, and rescuing. By this means the addicted person is allowed to progress more quickly through his own stages of recovery.

3. It provides your loved one with *his own* reason to enter treatment. The addicted person must have a compelling reason to start trying to get better, and it must be a personal reason. Because the exact nature and timing of that compelling reason is unpredictable, family members must begin to reclaim their own lives by focusing on health, happiness, and other family members.

4. It helps you to begin to rebuild boundaries, communication, and trust. Healthy boundaries are important for healthy families. Addiction creates a blur between your business as a parent or sibling and that which is not your business. This becomes increasingly evident as family members struggle to solve problems which are not their problems to solve. Once healthy boundaries start to solidify, a healthier form of communication can begin—one that is two-way, not focused on old problems, and not designed to manipulate or entice someone into changing one's behavior. This, in turn, will foster a beginning of trust. Family members will no longer be engaged in the old power-play of trying to control someone else; they will have ceased eliciting promises and confrontations that evoke lies and justifications.

Families can indeed create an environment of change by removing the safety net that protects their loved one from the mounting consequences created by the disease. There is no better intervention than for families to change, end their participation in their loved one's crises, and hasten his discovery of compelling reasons to get well.

+ + +

Chapter Highlights and Suggestions

- Because of the addiction, you're loved one can't keep promises

- An extracted promise means a broken promise

- Traditional interventions overemphasize the effectiveness of treatment and underemphasize the power of the family; they don't address rescuing and relationships and leave the family ill-prepared for post-treatment challenges

- Family process interventions focus on:
  o changing roles
  o abandoning rescuing
  o shifting the consequences to the addicted person
  o preparing your loved one for treatment and recovery
  o preparing the family for continued involvement
  o providing your loved one with *his own* reason to enter treatment

7) Avoid the Reactions of Anger and Pity

One young man told this story about the time he was in jail:

> I had big-time legal problems, I was broke, and I had no place to live. My father came to visit me in jail. He went on and on about my terrible behavior, how much I'd hurt Mom, how much money I'd cost them, and how many promises I'd broken. But to tell you the truth, I felt relieved. I knew as soon as he started yelling that everything was going to be all right. I knew right then that he was going to get me out of jail, let me live at home, and help me with the rest of my problems. Why else would he be yelling at me if he wasn't going to help me?

Anger and Pity

Anger is the easiest emotion for the addicted person to manipulate. When you get angry and raise your voice, your loved one will either (a) yell back, or (b) wait until you say something you shouldn't have said. Either way getting angry sets you up for failure and you'll end up apologizing. Moreover, you'll lose every argument because the addicted person doesn't argue fairly. For him, facts don't matter. Alcologic rules; his world is upside down. Everything and everybody else is to blame. It's like throwing paper into a fan. "After talking with Tom for twenty minutes, I felt like *I* was the one who was crazy."

For any given amount of anger directed toward the addicted individual, an equal amount of pity will follow. "We're not giving you any money!" is eventually succeeded by a loosening of the family purse strings. "I'm not getting you out of jail!" precedes bail money by an hour or a day or a week. Then the bargaining resumes. "OK, we'll help you this time but you have to promise that you'll...."

The challenge for the family is to realize that the offending behavior is only a symptom of the disease. Your addicted loved one is unable to consistently keep promises, show up on time, or be responsible. This isn't because he's a bad person or doesn't love his family. As the drug increasingly directs his behavior, his life goes out of control.

Family members desperately want their loved one to be normal so they look for any small piece of evidence that he's getting better. These expectations, however, only fuel the disappointment and anger that follow. Family members must approach addiction objectively and avoid emotional responses to the abnormal behaviors—the symptoms—of the disease.

Perspective and Priorities

The symptoms of the disease serve as distractions. Like stomping out brush fires while the entire forest is in flames, the family spends unnecessary amounts of time and energy working to solve individual crises instead of addressing the cause of the problem. This leads, of course, to excessive worry, an emotion that can itself produce emotional and physical stress. Worry, like anger, results in a loss of perspective.

As an example, a mother expressed concern over her adult daughter's drug addiction. She explained that the young woman was enrolled in college, a daily user of opiates, and a frequent binge drinker. Her daughter had repeatedly stolen money from the family and within the past year had been hospitalized for a drug overdose. In an effort to motivate the daughter toward treatment, the mother was presented with a strategy for a family intervention. The mother balked, complaining that going into treatment would force her daughter to drop out of school.

Missing a semester of college would matter little if the daughter's addiction could be addressed promptly. The completion of classes would suddenly shrink in significance if the daughter overdosed again. Yet such distorted priorities are common among families. Both the worrying associated with the perpetual recurrence of crises and the desire for things to appear normal cause a serious loss of perspective.

This inability to prioritize also plagues the addicted individual. Many times an addicted person will postpone entry into treatment to complete some perceived obligation. "I can't go to treatment because I have to work" or "I can't leave my kids." A powerful Alcoholics Anonymous slogan states, "Whatever you put ahead of your recovery will be the next thing you'll lose." Postponing treatment means the addiction will progress; the job and the kids will be lost anyway.

So anger results in pity and pity results in a distortion of perspective and priorities. These pitfalls can be avoided by focusing on the disease instead of its myriad misleading symptoms.

Chapter Highlights and Suggestions

- Your anger is the emotion most easily manipulated by your loved one

- Pity will inevitably follow your anger

- Your loved one's offensive behavior is only a symptom of his disease

- Worrying about each crisis is stressful and unproductive

- Maintain perspective by prioritizing events and goals

8) Don't Accommodate the Disease

Accommodating means adjusting and making room for the disease. When family members sacrifice plans, money, security, and happiness they are being held hostage. These changes occur subtly, evolve over an extended period, and reach unimaginable proportions.

Here are true examples of disease accommodation:

- a spouse set her alarm for one a.m. each night and then drove ten miles to extract her husband from a bar so he wouldn't receive a DUI

- parents stopped inviting guests to their house fearing that their addicted son would embarrass them

- parents locked up their money and valuables so their thirty-year-old son wouldn't steal from them

- a family sold its second car to pay the son's legal fees

- a married couple stopped taking vacations for several years fearing that their adult daughter would need something at home

- a mother did not sleep well for three years, afraid that her adult son would start a fire while drinking and smoking

Family members slowly and unknowingly make subtle changes in their lives to make room for the disease. The situation is described in the book by Marion H. Typpo, Ph.D., *An Elephant In The Living Room*. No one talks about it; it's there but it's ignored. Family members are tacitly saying, "How can we change *our* lives so the addicted person won't experience consequences and can keep on using?"

In dealing with disease accommodation and the skewed relationship with your loved one, first ask, "What sort of relationship did I expect to have when he was this age?" This starting point will reveal just how distorted your relationship has become.

Next, begin the process of becoming disentangled. As long as you're giving money, paying bills, or providing other support for your loved one's addiction, a healthy relationship will remain elusive. But as soon as you start disentangling, your anger subsides and things begin to improve.

Your loved one will no longer break promises because you've stopped extracting promises. Your loved one will not be wasting your money because you're not giving him any. And your loved one won't disappoint you as he once did because you aren't expecting him to act normal simply because he's not normal. During this period of adjustment, relief comes with unburdening. No longer are you forced to deal with your loved one's heartbreaking daily struggles.

You May See Less of Him

One sad reality of seeking this healthier relation-ship is that if you're no longer supporting your loved one's disease, he may no longer desire to associate with you. Many families find that once they stop rescuing, their loved one seems to disappear. He's lost interest in—and the need for—the relationship. Should he initiate contact again, it's usually an attempt to be rescued one more time. This is an opportunity for the family to say "no" (one more time) and to offer guidance toward getting help in the form of treatment. This, though an extremely difficult time for families, can be a turning point.

Just as addiction is progressive, so too is accommodation. However intrusive into your life the disease is today, tomorrow it will be worse. Initially your loved one's needs seemed manageable: a few dollars here and a small favor there. With time, however, the demands of the disease become unmanageable. Untreated addiction eventually strips the addicted person of everything, including his family's resources. Then accommodation is complete—the loved one's problems now belong to the family.

+ + +

Chapter Highlights and Suggestions

- The disease of addiction can hold the family hostage

- Don't make room for the disease

- Compare your current relationship with your loved one to the
  one you expected to have by now

- Start disentangling now

- When you disentangle, expect
  your loved one to become more
  distant

- Saying "no" one more time can be
  a turning point

9) Understand the Recovery Process

The immediate goal for family members—though not the end of the process—is to get their loved one into treatment. For this to happen the truth must have been confronted, consequences must have been experienced by the loved one, and the responsibility and blame for the consequences must have been allowed to shift from the family to their true source—the addicted individual. Only then will the addicted person consider quitting and entering treatment. But as we shall see, treatment is just the starting line.

Hitting Bottom

No one has ever entered recovery without first "hitting bottom," an often misunderstood term. As discussed earlier, to many people it means that the addicted individual must suffer to extremes. He must lose his car, his house, his family, and end up homeless or in jail.

But a "bottom" is not at the same place for everyone. "Bottoms" are those sets of circumstances, consequences, and painful emotional states that motivate the addicted person to accept help and become willing to begin recovery activities. For some, a bottom may only be the threat of loss, such as a job, spouse, or respect. For others, it may mean actual losses of property, relationships, or self-image. Sometimes the consequences are external, such as the loss of a job, family, or an accumulation of legal problems. Internal consequences, which are often kept hidden, include the emotions of guilt, shame, and self-pity.

Said another way, a bottom is that place in time when the individual is finally motivated to seek an alternative to his addicted lifestyle. Each person's bottom is in a different place but no bottom is in a good place. Here, consequences are being experienced. For family members, hopes may be building but uncertainties persist.

While for nearly every individual it's the convergence, or accumulation, of multiple consequences that motivates a decision to change, any single crisis can become anyone's personal bottom. Recovery often begins on the worst day of the addicted person's life. "It was my worst day—ever." Overcome by hopelessness and despair, a tiny chink in the armor of denial finally appears.

One of the descriptions of alcoholism is an elevator going down. The alcoholic can exit at any floor. If he doesn't, the elevator continues its path to the next floor, or to the next, more serious consequence. No one can predict which set of circumstances will provoke the decision to get off the elevator and move toward recovery, but one thing is certain: *The addicted person's bottom is always one crisis beyond the family's ability or willingness to fix it.*

Any point on the downward spiral can be your loved one's bottom if he is allowed to fully experience the consequences of his behavior. If anyone relieves some or all of the pain caused by the consequences, the addicted person will inevitably progress to the next—and worse—consequence.

This most difficult time for family members requires a form of love that is painful for everyone. They must have the willingness to allow their loved one to suffer the current consequence to avoid the next, more severe consequence. In AA this is known as "raising the bottom," and indicates that people need not experience more painful consequences if they are allowed to experience their current consequences. For family members this is an extreme act of love and unselfishness.

What Is Recovery?

Recovery is a process, not an event, and requires attention for a lifetime. There is the tendency to hope that one day your loved one will just quit drinking or using drugs and that will be that. Unfortunately, like asthma or diabetes, addiction is a chronic, lifelong condition. It can be arrested but it can't be cured. Families unable to understand and accept this reality become resentful, discouraged, and frustrated.

The primary focus of every continuing recovery program is on helping the person to attain and maintain abstinence, and to "grow up." Remember that emotional maturation virtually ceases once drug use begins. It follows, then, that much of recovery must emphasize the need to mature, take responsibility, and become an independent, drug-free individual.

Recovery is much more than not drinking or using drugs. AA old-timers often tell newcomers, "There's only one thing you'll need to change to stay sober for the rest of your life." The newcomer, anxious to learn of an easy road to recovery, asks, "What is that one thing?" To which the old-timer responds, "Everything."

That's not quite the case but it's close. To be successful the newcomer to recovery must be willing to examine closely all of his behaviors, relationships, and attitudes under the direction of an addiction professional and an AA or NA (Narcotics Anonymous) sponsor. Recovery from addiction is about accepting the realities of the disease and building a support system that does not depend on the family for help.

Not only must your newly recovering loved one deal with his current circumstances, he must also face the smoldering bridges of his past: damaged relationships, legal difficulties, or unresolved financial problems. It's essential that he confronts them, but with the guidance and assistance of the recovering community. The family and the addicted person must try to reclaim a balanced relationship where the family is no longer struggling to help the addicted individual. Continuation of the old relationship will not only prevent opportunities for new, healthy interactions but will also increase the chance of relapse.

➤ *Early Recovery*

Early recovery roughly includes the first year after attaining abstinence. Normal symptoms during this period include difficulty sleeping, restlessness, anger, and resentments. The recovering person is said to be *abstinent*, as opposed to *sober*. Abstinence means not using, sobriety means happily not using, and the distinction is not hair-splitting. Abstinence alone is not uncommon (see *Dry Drunk*, below). Only sobriety results in a productive human being capable of establishing deep, loving relationships. Sobriety occurs sometime during recovery. A valued promise of recovery is that at some point in the process the desire to drink or use drugs will disappear.

Treatment options, discussed in a later section, vary widely and may include inpatient, residential, counseling, intensive out-patient (IOP), out-patient, and 12-Step recovery.

During early recovery, it's a frequent and mistaken tendency for families to offer too much financial and material support. Support should be offered in the form of encouragement. Rescuing is just as futile and dangerous during recovery as it was when the addiction was active.

Family members should focus on and applaud change. If everything stays the same and the addicted person remains dependent on the family, progress is impossible. Also keep in mind that you can't say the wrong thing. You're not responsible for your loved one's recovery any more than you were responsible for his using. Avoid walking around on eggshells. Only rescuing can contribute to relapse.

Note that there's a difference between motivation and willingness. Motivation is what got your loved one into treatment; willingness is what will keep him there. Motivation, the starting point, results in that first entry into treatment or that first AA or NA meeting. Willingness, on the other hand, requires considerable time before becoming fully integrated and second-nature. A newly recovering alcoholic asked his sponsor, "How long do I have to go to these meetings?" The sponsor's perfect answer was, "Until you want to."

> ➤ *Vagaries of Recovery*

Recovery is a messy time for everyone. Your loved one is on a roller coaster of mood swings, worries, drug cravings, and physical discomfort. He's plagued by insomnia, dietary indiscretions, irritability, joylessness, and loss of enthusiasm. Family members are presented with a different loved one from one hour to the next. To ease this burden, families must keep in mind that there's nothing they can say or do that will cause their loved one to remain in recovery—or to relapse.

Once your loved one stops using drugs, health and happiness will be slow to return. Changes in brain chemistry resulted in a dependency on drugs to "feel good" and, if he reached the later stages of the disease, just to "feel normal." After removal of the drugs, while the brain begins to heal, he'll often feel bad or nothing. During this early, joyless period of recovery, it's important that your loved one interacts with other people in recovery. Only other recovering people, whose opinions are respected because of similar pasts, have the ability to convince the newcomer that he is going to be OK. Families should continue to be supportive, of course, but they're unable to empathize from a position of shared experience.

Even if the addicted person is not yet participating, families have much to gain by attending open meetings of Alcoholics Anonymous and Narcotics Anonymous. In addition to the opportunity to see "recovery in action," family members can form important relationships which can help them or their loved one later. And since family members often feel lost and hopeless, attendance at open meetings reveals a whole new atmosphere of optimism. People who were once just like your loved one (or worse) can be seen experiencing the life-changing world of recovery.

> *Dry Drunk*

This AA term, which refers to a condition where the addicted individual remains abstinent but un-happy, is applied at one time or another to most re-covering people. The dry drunk continues to be burdened with unresolved resentments, regrets, and fears. Because of stunted emotional development, he's judgmental of others (ironic considering his previous lifestyle). This condition is usually found in people who have quit using but are not addressing the new realities of sober living. The 12 Steps of AA and NA are specifically designed to assist the recovering per-son with these lingering problems through a process of personal growth. One promise of 12-Step programs, that a person "will not regret the past nor wish to shut the door upon it," indicates that one can build on past guilt and resentments and use them to help them-selves and others.

As recovery unfolds many, if not all, recovering people find they have additional issues that need to be addressed. These may be related to nutrition or health, marriage, parenting, or life development in general. Once sober, each recovering individual has a personal history which must be confronted—but only after first addressing his recovery from addiction.

Principles of Recovery

The following list of general principles of recovery is meant to clarify the concepts discussed above and may be applied to specific situations.

- The burden of recovery rests with the addict
- Recovery is about taking responsibility for:
  - making personal changes
  - building character
  - attaining balanced relationships
- Relapse, discussed below, is part of the recovery process
- Early recovery is dynamic and involves mistakes
- Recovery requires incorporation of behaviors and attitudes not initially accepted
- Anything considered more important than recovery creates a risk of relapse
- New sexual relationships in early recovery are a risk to recovery
- Your recovering loved one will not be the person he was during his active addiction, but he will probably not be the person you expected, either; he will be a new person
- Early recovery is work; continued recovery is a joy
- Remaining with dry people in dry places is important during early recovery; long-term recovery with the guidance of a sponsor will allow the recovering person to fully participate in the world without being concerned if alcohol or drugs are present

- Recovery consists of activities that the addicted person *must* do until he *wants* to
- AA and NA offer the most promising and available programs for lifelong recovery support
- With true recovery comes complete freedom from the desire to drink or use
- Recovery introduces a new purpose: to help others

Getting Ready For Recovery

What follows are specific activities that can educate and prepare families *before* their loved one enters recovery:

- **Investigate the treatment programs in your community.** Making contact with a specific facility will not only create an ally for family guidance, but will also become a resource toward which you can direct your loved one. As you become disentangled from his chaotic world of addiction, you can divert his requests for help to the treatment program's contact phone number.

- **Attend open AA or NA meetings.** These meetings are open to the public and provide an excellent place for family members to learn about addiction and recovery. The stories, or "leads," of recovering people bring under-standing, direction, and hope. You'll hear things like, "My family quit helping, I experienced consequences, I got angry, and now I'm thanking them for saving my life."

- **Attend Al-Anon meetings.** Al-Anon may be the most powerful resource at this point. Recommended for family members who are attempting to make the necessary changes in their lives, this organization provides support while weathering the emotional storms of addiction. Al-Anon is essentially Alcoholics Anonymous for families. The information you receive from this book is helpful but putting the suggestions into practice is difficult. By sharing experiences, Al-Anon provides families with the strength to say "no" as their loved one struggles with addiction.

Recovery Is a Process

Like the disease of addiction itself, recovery can be broken down into basic phases: controlling, quitting for awhile, quitting with "his" plan, and quitting with someone else's plan. Recovery almost always begins with:

> ➤ *Controlling*

Attempts to control the use of drugs or alcohol begin early in the course of the addicted individual's disease and may actually be present at the start. Long before family, friends, employers, or counselors try to intervene, the addicted person has already fought many losing battles with the drug. While normal people have no need to exert control, it's necessary for the addicted individual. His purpose for controlling is to minimize the consequences without giving up his drug use entirely.

An addicted person will employ many methods to exercise control. He'll try to control the frequency ("I won't use until five o'clock"), the amount ("No more than a six-pack a day"), or the type of drug. He may quit alcohol and switch back to marijuana (the "marijuana maintenance" program). The crack-addicted person may take up alcohol again. Or the person on opiates may look to benzodiazepines in an attempt to thwart the mounting consequences. And often he'll try to make behavioral changes: "I'll never drink and drive" or "I'll never miss work because of drinking" or "I'll never use around my kids."

The decision to control may also involve certain "geographical" changes such as leaving town, changing friends and relationships, or switching jobs. To the addicted person's delight, family members often get drawn in and support these changes. Eventually, however, he discovers that, "Everywhere I went I took me with me." In the end no changes actually occur, and the use continues as before.

When your loved one first started using alcohol or drugs he had no idea that their use would consume his life or involve all his activities. Most addicted people have moments of clarity when they ask themselves, "How did I get in this shape? How did I get to this point?" The addicted person, of course, is unaware of his powerlessness. As he continues to try to control his use and his disease progresses, he breaks every promise he makes. From repeated efforts to control he eventually becomes emotionally devastated, a state that results in frustration, anger, and denial.

The controlling addicted person also faces the dangers of *cross addiction*. Becoming abstinent from one drug does not grant immunity to others. Once the brain's addictive process is under way, any addictive substance creates the risk of a new addiction. Many relapses occur because the addicted individual believed that after quitting cocaine, for example, it was safe to use alcohol. He then soon experienced either out-of-control drinking or renewed cocaine cravings. One person recovering from crack cocaine, after being readmitted to a treatment facility, noted, "It's damn hard to quit using crack and stay quit, and it's impossible to quit crack when you're drunk."

So as efforts to control the amount, type, frequency, and situations of drug use continue to fail, as the consequences mount, and as family conflicts deepen, the addicted person will probably try:

➤ *Quitting For A While*

Like attempts to control, the decision to quit on one's own is kept secret. Avoiding the shame of failure clearly indicates there is no intention to quit permanently. This quitting-for-a-while decision also involves a promise, such as, "I'll quit until my family thinks better of me" or "I'll quit until my finances get straightened out" or "I'll quit until I'm on better terms at work." The addicted person may successfully relieve himself of existing problems but the drug use invariably resumes. Consequences re-accumulate and the cycle begins again: promise → quit → resume → consequences.

It should be noted that quitting and then restarting has no effect on the disease. The disease progresses even while the addicted person is not using. Upon resumption of use, it's as if he'd never quit; he's immediately out of control again.

So the addicted person's first effort to quit is only temporary. He's not quitting forever; he only wants to repair some damage, heal some relationships, or get out of trouble. Once he gets over the hump—pays off his debts, gets healthy, and reforms relationships—he plans to use again. The next time around will be better, his denial system tells him, and things won't get out of hand again.

For unaware family members, this seems like a time for rejoicing. Their loved one is not using and appears to be getting his life in order. During this dangerously misleading "rally point," the family may invest additional resources in the form of cash, rent, a vehicle, college tuition, or legal fees. The family believes the "bad phase" is over and offers all kinds of support. But without knowledge of the nature of the disease and without professional help, relapse is inevitable. The addicted person's only motivation to abstain was to avoid a current or impending crisis. The family becomes terribly angry and disappointed all over again.

Disillusioned after many futile efforts to control and several false starts toward abstinence, the addicted person will move on to the next phase of recovery, one that may be omitted entirely:

> *Quitting With "His" Plan*

Your loved one's plan to quit demonstrates progress but is doomed to failure because it's the brainchild of his own chemically confused brain. His plan usually includes some elements consistent with an acceptable approach to recovery but omits others that are essential for success, such as counseling, treatment, or 12-Step programs. Desperate to see recovery begin, his plan initially appeals to family members because it involves quitting so, once again, they happily succumb to the promises of success.

A fundamental flaw in the addicted person's plan is that it requires someone else's resources. "Mom and Dad, I'm going to quit using and move back home for a while." "I'm going to a methadone clinic (see *Replacement Therapy, Methadone*) but I need you to pay for it." "Can you give me money for that detox program?" "If you could just help me with my rent and let me use your car, I'm going to quit, start going to church, and get a job."

Your loved one will continue to try to make his plan succeed as long as the family continues to supply the resources for it or until continued consequences force him to abandon his plan. And this is why it's often possible to omit or significantly reduce the time spent in this stage of recovery: if his plan is not supported it will fail.

For a while, continued lack of success (meaning relapse) doesn't discourage him. He believes that his plan is the correct plan and that it failed only because he didn't try hard enough, someone else ruined it, or bad luck intervened. When family members continue to allow themselves to experience the consequences of the failures of his plan, he'll keep trying over and over. Or, if the family analyzes and attacks his plan, he'll actually become more motivated to persist in his attempts; arguing about his plan won't work.

On the bright side, movement into this phase of recovery reveals that your loved one has a limited but growing awareness that he cannot use alcohol or drugs and that abstinence might have to be forever. (Not to be confused with AA's "one day at a time" concept, wherein "forever" to the recovering person implies that his disease is permanent and that abstinence must be a lifelong goal, fulfilled one day at a time.)

If family members approach his plan correctly, they can turn the failures into motivators. But first the family must get out of the way. Then, when the plan doesn't work, they won't be affected. "I hope your plan works, but we're not going to participate in it because your plan doesn't include treatment." To become motivated toward recovery, the addicted person must feel the results of the failure of his plan.

Eventually your loved one will either experience a sufficient number of consequences using "his" plan and give up, or the family will withdraw its support. He'll then finally have the willingness to progress to the last stage of recovery which consists of:

➢ *Quitting With Someone Else's Plan*

At this stage your loved one has reached a place of greater open-mindedness. Either he has a growing awareness that his plan is only leading to escalating consequences, or he's unable to access the resources needed to continue with his plan.

This new level of open-mindedness affords your loved one with an opportunity to accept suggestions and guidance from those who have demonstrated a history of success in dealing with addiction. For some this involves a plan developed by a professional addiction counselor; for others the plan may be suggested by a successful member of AA or NA.

Family members need not try to measure the amount of acceptance and motivation. More important is your loved one's willingness to listen and follow through with the suggestions made by those who know how to get sober and stay sober. Action on his part is the key ingredient, and this action must be directed by an outside resource with a time-tested plan for recovery.

Also at this stage your loved one has finally reached his personal bottom, or motivating experience, where the consequences have begun to outweigh the chemical high. That WOW experience has become elusive; the highs aren't as high anymore. Physical addiction is present and withdrawal symptoms are surfacing. His use has brought him to that dreadful place where he's both unable to imagine life without drugs and unable to imagine life with drugs. He has painted himself into the worst of all possible corners. He has reached an unbearable condition of joylessness.

From this point on, every response to any melodramatic call for rescuing should point to a community recovery facility with which you are familiar. "We love you but we can't help you. Here is someone who can." You've successfully stopped rescuing, but he's not yet in recovery. The question now is: "How well can you wait?"

When you begin responding with detachment, your loved one probably won't react immediately. And if you consistently react by indicating treatment instead of yourself as a source for help, it's likely he'll become irritated. Don't waste your time trying to talk your loved one into treatment. He won't respond to words; threatening, cajoling, and reasoning won't work. Because an addicted person is unable to keep promises, this is no time for negotiating. Even if he agrees to go into treatment if you rescue him "this one last time," he won't follow through.

So when your loved one finally decides to quit with someone else's plan he's becoming open-minded. Most often the decision arises from the desire to avoid future consequences. Sometimes the consequences are external, such as choosing treatment to avoid jail, and sometimes they're internal, because of, say, the emergence of withdrawal symptoms. "I'm sick and tired of being sick and tired" is a common refrain. But beneath it all is the irrefutable knowledge that next time he won't be rescued.

> I had tried to quit drinking and using drugs a number of times. I was somewhat successful a couple of times, briefly, but it always turned out the same. I'd use again and then be mystified as to how I ended up back where I started, or worse. I had made the rounds of the outpatient programs, methadone clinics, and church programs. I even got my family to pay for an expensive 'rapid detox' program that didn't work.

On two occasions counselors told me that I needed residential treatment followed by regular AA or NA meeting attendance. Of course I rejected this advice both times, thinking I wasn't that bad, that I could control it on my own, or that I couldn't possibly spend all that time in treatment and meetings.

I remember approaching my family about getting their financial support to make another go at the methadone program. To my surprise they said no. I was pretty upset and tried to make them feel guilty. I even told them that they'd be to blame for whatever bad things happened to me. But they stood firm.

One day out of desperation I called the last treatment program I'd been in— one of the ones that had recommended residential treatment—and asked for their help. I was pretty sick—not just physically but in the head too. I remember trying to bargain with the counselor about how much treatment I needed. He told me that the definition of insanity is doing the same thing over and over again and expecting different results. Reluctantly I accepted his recommendation for residential treatment.

It was really hard waiting for a bed to become available. Each day I wavered back and forth about my decision and of course I continued to use. It took a couple of weeks for all the arrangements to come together. When my admission day came I was pretty much ready to go; I'd given up.

In hindsight it was the best decision I'd made in a very long time. It didn't seem much like a decision at the time but I'd run out of options. Even after I got into treatment I was resistant to their suggestions. But over time I started getting well and the suggestions got easier. I found myself actually going to more AA and NA meetings than required. I guess that's when I knew something really good was happening to me.

The Family's Role in Recovery

➤ *Let Recovery Happen*

Now that someone else's plan has been accepted, the family must take a back seat for a while. The responsibility for actually obtaining help must shift to the loved one; the family is not the "recovery police." At this point the more family members help their loved one into recovery, the less he will do on his own to recover. Your loved one is giving up old ideas and listening to a new plan, one that usually originates with someone already in recovery. The beginning may be as simple as a phone call to a treatment facility or to find out the time and place of the next AA meeting.

Once your loved one begins the recovery process, he must be allowed to grow up. This means permitting his battered self-esteem time to regain its composure. And because self-esteem is improved largely through accomplishments, it's essential that the recovering person be left alone to find his way back into the world without an over-abundance of assistance.

Also, the family must be wary of rewarding the recovering loved one with material goods; instead, let him earn his way back. Remember that when he started using drugs his emotional maturation came to a halt. He used drugs to cope with difficulties instead of allowing the difficulties to bring about maturity. Counselors and sponsors, not the family, are best suited to facilitate the maturation process.

> An adult daughter had struggled with addiction for years. Each time she got sober her father rewarded her. Once he gave her a car, another time it was cash, and more than once he paid her back rent. Fearing that being faced with difficulties would make her return to drugs, he wanted to make life as easy as possible for her. But invariably she relapsed.
>
> Frustrated, her father finally gave up and washed his hands of the situation. Months later she was sober, holding down a decent job, and driving a used car that she had purchased herself. She said later that she appreciated her father's earlier efforts to help but was more proud of her old car than anything he had given her. "I earned it," she said.

Although your loved one may want to retain the earlier roles at least for a while, it's time for the family to reclaim the relationship and get out of the role. A mother, for example, was taking care of her daughter's children after driving her daughter to NA meetings. Then, after she learned of a more helpful behavior, she began insisting that her daughter find her own transportation and that she would baby-sit only on certain days of the week.

> *Family Support*

How can the family be helpful once the recovery process has started? Always remember that the family's withdrawal of support was a powerful motivating factor in the addicted person's decision to begin recovery in the first place. Don't drift back into rescuing and taking care of him. Early recovery largely depends on maintaining the motivating factors that caused him to stop using and get help. If the negative consequences are removed prematurely, relapse is next.

> A spouse finally gave up and left her alcoholic husband. For him, losing his family was the negative consequence— his personal bottom—that motivated him to enter recovery. He got sober, entered treatment, and began attending daily AA meetings. After a while, his wife succumbed to his urgings and returned home. He soon began missing counseling appointments and AA meetings and within a few weeks, secretively at first, he was drinking again.

Remember that your goal in dealing with your addicted loved one—both when his disease was active and now that he's in recovery—is to normalize your relationship by ceasing to rescue and becoming disentangled. Your efforts should be directed at reclaiming an appropriate, healthy relationship.

Since the disease of addiction creates an unhealthy rescuing dynamic within the family, it's important to identify some of the characteristics of a healthy family recovery environment.

Helpful family members should:

- view addiction as a disease, not a character weakness
- understand that relapse is often a part of recovery
- respect the recovering individual's priorities in the presence of drinking and drug use
- understand the ramifications of enabling
- become willing to forgive past wrongs and conflicts
- seek to develop a normal relationship with the loved one
- obtain guidance from professionals or concerned family groups
- support the independence of the loved one

A common question is, "How can I know for sure that he's serious about quitting drugs and alcohol?" The answer is simple: you can't be sure. If he seems overly optimistic about his recovery, beware; it's likely that he's using recovery as a pretext to get something else from you. People making honest attempts at recovery will show a modicum of humility and won't make bold, overconfident statements about their progress. For some degree of proof of your loved one's good intentions, look to his actions. Is he staying sober? Is he engaged in an intensive treatment program? Is he going to AA or NA meetings? Is he *not* asking you for money or favors as if everything has been forgotten and all is well?

Early recovery is a confusing time for everyone, especially the recovering person. While he's motivated enough to be in recovery, he's also struggling to perform all the suggested activities that will ensure success. He wants to grow up and at the same time wants the security of family resources. He wants to be independent and also have the nicer things in life without working for them. Some days he seems like a brand new person and other days he appears to be his old, misguided self.

Addicted individuals enter recovery primarily because of one motivating influence—the consequences of their use. Over time, the motivation can turn into willingness. The AA old-timer's admonition that the newcomer will have to attend meetings until he wants to embodies this reality. What begins as a list of required recovery activities eventually becomes a collection of desirable experiences. For the sincere recovering person, attending meetings and helping others stay sober become enjoyable and rewarding.

So let your loved one take responsibility for his own recovery. Many addicted people are immature and will want you to act as a protective shield in their recovery activities, such as attending meetings with them, but this is self-defeating. Let him keep track of meeting schedules and counseling appointments. If your loved one has lost his driving privileges and transportation to meetings is an issue, indicate a date beyond which he must provide his own transportation. Your loved one was extremely resourceful when he was looking for drugs; insist that he apply that same ingenuity to accessing his own recovery.

Encouragement comes from positive signs of improvement. You can be quite certain that your loved one is making progress in recovery if he is:

- taking responsibility by making fewer requests for your help
- making new, supportive, recovering friends
- moving up and down on early recovery's emotional roller coaster
- consistently attending AA or NA meetings
- talking less often about the same old problems and difficulties
- exhibiting less selfishness and self-centeredness
- making amends that go beyond saying "I'm sorry"
- reclaiming an adult relationship with family members

The addicted person in early recovery, trying to avoid the simmering conflicts of the past, will find open communication with the family difficult or even impossible at first. Previous discussions centered on crises and rescue, so finding new, untainted subject matter can be problematic. In any event, your recovering loved one should not be bringing his current problems to you. He should be addressing his concerns to a counselor or sponsor. The family does not possess the expertise to help a recovering person with his recovery struggles.

Treatment Services

Most addicted people enter treatment voluntarily, usually with the support of family, friends, or co-workers. Some are court-ordered and have a history of criminal behavior. Overall, the type of treatment depends on the nature and severity of the addiction, the addicted person's motivation, and the availability of services.

Two factors have been shown to correlate with good recovery outcomes:

1. Length of treatment: The longer the addicted person remains engaged in the treatment process, the better his chance for recovery. Beware of programs that offer a "quick fix." While both the addicted person and the family want a rapid recovery, there is no easy, short-cut method.

2. AA or NA involvement: People who commit themselves to regular 12-Step meeting attendance have improved recovery outcomes. Quitting drug use is only the first step toward recovery; AA and NA provide superior environments to continue the process.

Choosing a treatment provider is paramount and can be difficult. It's important to locate a comprehensive program capable of offering a full continuum of care, which includes detoxification, residential, outpatient, and aftercare. Also highly recommended is a facility that values the programs of Alcoholics Anonymous and Narcotics Anonymous.

Ask the program to provide outcome data to assess the recidivism rate. On admission the facility should check for concurrent diseases (co-morbidities) and HIV risk. Shock-type therapy, such as interventions with yelling, should not be a part of a legitimate treatment program. If your addicted loved one is a teenager, certain unique needs must be addressed. (Adolescent addiction specialist Michael Dennis, Ph.D., jokingly describes adolescence as a "borderline personality disorder.") Only centers with separate facilities for adults and adolescents are acceptable.

A Recommended Treatment Plan

While numerous treatment and recovery agendas are being offered by countless individuals and facilities, the plan outlined below is based upon what has worked best for a large number of people over a significant period of time. If you were to visit your doctor for the treatment of cancer, you'd expect a regimen that would give you the best chance for recovery. No promises or guarantees are possible with any form of treatment, but the plan described here offers opportunities for success for the majority of addicted individuals.

➤ *Detoxification*

Professional intervention should begin with an evaluation to determine the need for detoxification, or "detox." An addiction professional assesses the potential for dangerous withdrawal and prescribes a course of treatment. In some cases inpatient detox may be necessary.

Withdrawal from certain drugs, such as alcohol and benzodiazepines, can be life-threatening and must be monitored. Withdrawal from cocaine presents some physical discomfort, but cravings can be overwhelming; "coming down" from cocaine can result in severe depression and restlessness.

Opiate withdrawal, which is physically uncomfortable and also accompanied by severe cravings, is ordinarily not harmful physically. The opiate-addicted person's fear of the symptoms of withdrawal, however, may present a significant barrier to abstaining and entering the recovery process. These symptoms can be alleviated almost entirely with Suboxone, a partial opioid substitute (see *Replacement Therapy*, below).

Another obstacle to recovery is the mistaken idea that a few days of detox will solve everything. Instead of following through with counseling and 12-Step programs, both vital to successful recovery, the focus is on withdrawal-abating medications such as Suboxone or methadone. Unfortunately, some physicians provide these medications to individuals addicted to opiates without making the essential referral to a treatment program.

➤ Level of Care

Once the need for detoxification has been assessed, the treatment professional should recommend a specific level of care. That determination is based on the stage of disease progression, life circumstances, ability to maintain abstinence, accessibility to services, and motivation. Least intensive are outpatient services, which are indicated for those able to participate in treatment while living within the neighboring community. Typically, regular outpatient sessions are held weekly while intensive outpatient (IOP) sessions meet three or four times a week. Inpatient (hospital) and residential treatment represent more intense levels of care; the addicted individual resides within a treatment facility for a specified period.

➤ Aftercare

Aftercare services are essential to the recovery process. As we come to fully appreciate the protracted nature of the disease of addiction, ongoing supportive treatment plays an increasingly vital role in successful outcomes. Seek a program that offers long-term opportunities for your loved one to remain connected to helpful professionals. Should relapse occur, this frightening (albeit normal) event can be kept in perspective by experienced aftercare and 12-Step personnel. Prompt re-entry into the recovering community is more likely if professionals and recovering AA and NA members are in close proximity.

Replacement Therapy

During the first seven days after abstaining from opiates, severe withdrawal symptoms may include muscle spasms, sweating, diarrhea, and cramping. These markedly uncomfortable complaints, accompanied by psychological and physical cravings, called being "dope sick," or "jonesing," often lead to relapse. One of the worst culprits is Oxycontin, which may prolong the withdrawal symptoms for a month or more. Although described below, pharmaceutical approaches alone are ineffective; they must be combined with an appropriate level of addiction treatment and counseling.

➤ *Methadone*

One withdrawal-avoidance method uses methadone, a full opiate substitute. Authorized clinics dispense methadone daily to prevent full-blown opiate withdrawal. However, because methadone produces its own (albeit lesser) high, some individuals merely use methadone to supplement their existing habits. And even normally dosed maintenance clients reach drug levels that make future detoxification from methadone extremely difficult. Withdrawal from methadone is reportedly more severe than heroin.

➤ *Suboxone*

Outpatient replacement therapy with the non-addictive drug buprenorphine (Suboxone) also alleviates the symptoms of acute withdrawal. But because it's only a partial opiate substitute, Suboxone does not produce significant euphoria. Also, because of Suboxone's "ceiling effect," excessive ingestion will not produce an overdose. Candidates for Suboxone detoxification must agree to comply strictly with the clinic's protocol and be willing to simultaneously enter a treatment program.

Drug Courts

First established in Miami-Dade County, Florida, in 1989, and now comprising nearly two thousand programs, drug courts are effective deterrents to relapse and re-arrest. These alternatives to incarceration for first-offense, nonviolent drug felons generally function to supervise long-term treatment as follows:

If your loved one is arrested for committing a low-level felony for the first time, he may be offered a choice of appearing before a judge for sentencing or entering the local drug court. (Given the choice, virtually everyone opts for drug court in lieu of jail time.)

Following a thirty-day observation period during which weekly urine drug screens and pre-sentence investigations are performed, a drug court team, consisting of a judge, parole officer, prosecutor and treatment representative, votes to allow (or not allow) your loved one to begin drug court. Restitution is also a requirement for admission to the court.

The complete oversight program lasts twelve to fifteen months and requires regular court appearances, urine testing, outpatient treatment, and AA or NA meeting attendance. Drug court violations are dealt with swiftly and sternly. Failure to appear, positive ("dirty") urine samples, or curfew violations may result in dismissal from the court and jail. At the graduation ceremony, the felony charge is dismissed. The judge may also expunge the client's record, leaving no trace of the prior offense.

According to a 2005 National Drug Court Institute report, "the Government Accountability Office concluded that adult drug court programs substantially reduce crime by lowering re-arrest and conviction rates among drug court graduates well after program completion, providing overall greater cost/benefits for drug court participants and graduates than comparison group members."

Insurance Woes

Discrimination by health insurance companies creates difficulties for addicted people motivated to recover. Either the insurance does not cover the disorder or large co-pays and deductibles make it impossible to afford. Managed care has reduced the amount, quality, and duration of addiction treatment more than any other area of care. More than forty percent of people seeking treatment cite cost as a barrier.

For example, a father who carried employer-sponsored health insurance for nearly twenty years attempted to get treatment for his teenage daughter who was suffering from addiction. Every treatment facility that he approached told him that his insurance policy provided such limited coverage that he would be personally responsible for thousands of dollars of the bill.

In relative terms, addiction treatment is inexpensive compared to treatment for other illnesses. The cost of treating cancer or heart disease, for example, is many times higher. The expense of a two-day hospital stay for a gall bladder removal would pay for months of facility-based addiction treatment.

For every dollar that is "saved" by not insuring addiction, thousands are spent on its consequences. Left untreated, addiction costs employers billions of dollars in lost productivity, accidents, and related expenses. And billions more are spent treating addiction-related health issues.

Relapse

Families must realize that relapse—the resumption of drinking or using drugs—is often part of the recovery process. If your loved one instead had cancer, you would hope that his treatment program would cure his disease. But with a recurrence you would not blame him or be angry with him. You would immediately focus on restarting his treatment, knowing that check-ups will be necessary for the remainder of his life.

The same attitude should be maintained when dealing with addiction. The occurrence of a relapse is not a time for blame or anger. Your loved one has a lifelong disease and must remain attentive to those things that increase the risk of relapse. Immediately re-engaging in treatment and increasing the intensity of support systems are the only appropriate responses.

Because of the risk of relapse, the recovering person should never entirely end his relationship with treatment and AA or NA. Even if he's involved only as a volunteer or peer support provider, not only is it more likely that he'll remain sober but, if a relapse should occur, it will be easier to get help and quickly back on track. (Ironically, at one time it was common for treatment programs to expel clients who had relapsed because they had "failed" or "misbehaved." In retrospect, those people were being punished for experiencing a part of the very disease for which they were supposedly being treated.)

Most addicted individuals will relapse after their first time in treatment and most relapses occur during the first three to nine months of recovery. Becoming re-engaged in a life left behind is stressful. The neglected job, the ignored children, and the buried debts must be faced in the new light of day. And amidst all of this, there remains the most difficult task of all: growing up.

As noted, emotional maturation ceases when the addiction begins. The addicted person may grow and develop in other ways—he may succeed in school, become an executive in a company, or write a book— but his emotional maturity stagnates. "My son is thirty-five going on sixteen."

Relapse, as part of the disease of addiction, is basically due to a lack of understanding of power-lessness. Relapse does not mean that the addicted person is no longer recovering; it can be viewed as a valuable teacher if it's accompanied by the resulting consequences, causing the addicted person to ask, "What is it that I need to do differently?"

With addiction, the brain's dopamine system, which normally activates our pleasure centers, is "hijacked" by drugs. When the brain is supplied by outside sources of dopamine stimulation (via drugs), it "forgets" how to produce the chemical itself. Then, when the drugs are withdrawn during a period of abstinence, the brain is unable to respond to otherwise pleasure-providing situations such as food or sex or a trip to the zoo. The addicted brain recalls that drugs produced an unequalled high and so begins craving the drug in its absence. This inability to receive pleasure from normal events, called *anhedonia,* produces boredom, restlessness, and anxiety—primary causes of relapse.

Warning signs of relapse include returning to relationships with using friends, breaking established rules, not explaining absences, becoming argumentative, and staying in secluded locations. Diminished attendance in recovery activities, such as outpatient treatment, counseling sessions, and AA meetings, represent red flags for an impending relapse. Prevention of relapse is difficult but it's clear that the longer the recovering person remains engaged in treatment or follow-up at some level, the more likely he is to remain sober. It's also known that if a relapse occurs, it's best to immediately return to treatment.

➤ *Drug Testing*

Drug (urine) testing can be a helpful tool for both the family and the addicted person. By providing a level of accountability, testing can be supportive to someone seeking sobriety and recovery. When initiated by the family, testing is usually carried out within the context of a recovery "contract," whereby the family requires testing in return for something offered to the loved one, such as a place to live. "You may live with us as long as you are not using and are participating in a recovery program. We will use drug testing to determine your sobriety."

An alternative inclusion in such a contract might require the loved one to sign a release of information with the treatment agency. This would allow the family to obtain progress reports that reveal whether the loved one is in compliance with treatment recommendations.

While testing is often utilized by treatment programs, various drug testing kits are also available to the public. Before requiring any drug testing, however, the family must decide what actions will be taken if the loved one fails (tests positive) and—most importantly—to follow through with those actions.

Hope

For the family, recovery is dynamic and not always pleasant. Even with the loved one safely in recovery, the family will continue to experience discomfort as he wakes up to previously ignored problems: old habits, guilt, shame, conflict, anger, and resentments. And because the family is a safe place for these new feelings to emerge, the family takes the brunt of it all and the loved one may actually appear worse. Now he's dealing with life on life's terms without chemical buffering. The family requires understanding, tolerance and, above all, patience.

For the recovering loved one, hope cannot be instilled by the family. Hope, meaning viewing the future as being full of positive possibilities, comes from the stories told by people who are solidly in recovery. The family is the last place for any sense of the addicted person's "wellness" to emerge. Both the family and the loved one in recovery must be patient and wait for good things to happen, comforted by the knowledge that good things *will* happen, one day at a time.

+ + +

Chapter Highlights and Suggestions

- "Hitting bottom" means reaching a place—because of painful personal consequences—where the addicted individual is motivated to seek help and begin recovery activities

- Recovery is a process and requires a lifetime of attention

- The focus of recovery is on changing and growing up

- Recovery means moving from abstinence (or dry drunk) to sobriety

- Early recovery is a roller coaster of emotions

- Families need to prepare for recovery

- The steps of recovery lead to quitting with someone else's plan

- Families should applaud change but allow their loved one to recover on his own

- A treatment provider should offer detoxification, residential, outpatient, and aftercare services

- Relapse is part of the recovery process—expect it

- Early recovery is work; continued recovery is a joy

- Good things *will* happen, one day at a time

10) Reclaim Your Own Life

Addiction takes people hostage. Hobbies, jobs, health, vacations, and other family members become secondary while the tornado of addiction whirls through the family. "I can't do anything else until this addiction problem is solved."

Addiction causes your loved one to become increasingly self-centered and the continuing drama is made to order. The last thing he wants is for the family to return to normal. As discussed earlier, this conflict, or triangulation, works for the addicted person because it lessens the likelihood that his addiction will be addressed. Shifting attention away from the addicted person amounts to an experienced consequence.

So although it may feel selfish, surprise the addicted individual. Go to a movie. Resume your hobby. Take a vacation. This will not only increase the addicted person's chance of entering recovery but it will also improve your own emotional health and provide an opportunity to reconcile intra-family differences. Reclaim what is rightfully yours: your own life.

The following passage, from a letter written by a father whose daughter was suffering from anorexia nervosa, illustrates the importance of not rescuing and maintaining one's own life:

> If your daughter is struggling for life in a raging torrent, you do not save her by jumping into the torrent with her, which

leads only to your both drowning together. Instead, you keep your feet on
the dry bank—you maintain as best you
can your own inner peace, the best and
strongest of who you are—and from that
solid ground reach out a rescuing hand.
"Mind your own business" means but-
ting out of other people's lives because
in the long run they must live their lives
for themselves, but it also means pay
mind to your own life, your own health
and wholeness, both for your own sake
and ultimately for the sake of those you
love too. Take care of yourself so you
can take care of them. A bleeding heart
is of no help to anybody if it bleeds to
death.

Entanglements

As the addiction progresses the family becomes
entangled in all aspects of the addicted person's life.
Emotional entanglements, especially, waste enormous
amounts of energy. Trying to solve the "problem of
the day" becomes a focal point for the family. Physical
entanglements, such as allowing the addicted one to
live at home or providing his transportation, similarly
test the family's tolerance.

But perhaps most devastating are financial entanglements, which can drain family resources. Well-
intentioned but misguided couples have sold their
second cars and taken out second mortgages hoping to
solve the financial nightmares created by their son's or
daughter's addiction. Keep in mind that most of the

money given to the addicted person will go toward maintaining his addiction—often straight to the drug dealer. He may claim that he needs cash for car repairs, groceries or rent, but be forewarned that his addiction is at the top of his list of things to pay for.

Addiction affects certain family members by stealing the mental and emotional attention previously given to others. Primary rescuers, for example, spend far more time than they realize thinking, worrying, and talking about their loved one. These activities may become so obsessive that the primary rescuer is unaware of the effect it's having on other family members who, in turn, feel neglected and become resentful. They may resist viewing the addicted person as having a disease and instead become angry at his monopoly of the rest of the family.

Because of the neglect resulting from the excessive attention given to the addicted person, some family relationships will require nurturing to heal the hurt that accumulated over time. It's important to talk openly about your experiences and how you've been affected. Although the process may be lengthy, focus especially on how your relationship with them has suffered. Apologies alone go only so far. Family members will want to see real change before they risk serious, in-depth discussions with you.

Venting years of frustration from being neglected, an adult daughter confessed to her mother that she hated her addicted sister:

> I got good grades, never got in trouble, never asked for extra money, worked to help pay for college, graduated at the top of my class, participated in high

school and college sports, but your mind
was always on my sister.

She recounted numerous occasions when her
sister's crises had prevented her from receiving justified
recognition. Because she was aware that her mother
was preoccupied, the daughter reached a point where
she would not even attempt to share her feelings or
accomplishments. She even resented the family counseling sessions because "all anybody wanted to talk
about was my addicted sister."

Marriages, as well, suffer greatly when the child is
using drugs or alcohol. Addiction divides and con-
quers. Disagreements centering on the correct course
of action often escalate into serious conflicts that
threaten all areas of the marital relationship:
communication, closeness, sex, and commitment. To
whatever degree one partner rescues, the other will
often offset the effort by rigidly refusing to help, and
criticizing the rescuer only increases the motivation to
rescue.

While it's unrealistic to expect all family members
to be on the same page at the same time, a reasonable
goal is to attempt to move closer together. The initial
step in this direction must be taken by the primary rescuer. When that person finds it within himself to start
the process of ceasing to take care of the addicted
loved one, other family members will begin to shed
their anger and rigidity.

When your loved one finally seeks help and begins
the recovery process, his prospects will be enhanced if
the family has created a healthy recovery environment
where rescuing is no longer an option and personal
responsibility is esteemed. Instead of being viewed as

a needy, handicapped person, he should be treated as an equal. Family members can express forgiveness while remaining tuned to the realities of addiction. A healthy family "minds its own business" and does not intrude upon the loved one's struggles and challenges. A healthy family recognizes its limitations in helping and focuses instead on communicating encouragement and love.

We highly recommend Al-Anon Family Groups for assisting families in their efforts to change and heal. While Al-Anon focuses on the need to stop rescuing, equally important is the emphasis it places on accepting the help of others.

Many family members, after considering our suggestions, discover that saying "no" to their loved one (and not rescuing) is easier said than done. At this point they can begin to share their experience of powerlessness over their loved one just as the loved one has been experiencing powerlessness over his addiction. In both instances, the disease of addiction has markedly lessened the ability to say "no." Like AA, Al-Anon Family Groups offer 12-Step assistance in dealing with this powerlessness. As one family member noted, "I found out *what* to do in the Loved Ones Group and I became *able to do it* through the support of Al-Anon."

Family members may also benefit from individual or family counseling. Knowledgeable addiction professionals can guide confused family members through the mesh of addiction's entanglements.

It's essential that family members get on with their lives now. Because no one can predict when the loved one will seek help and begin recovery, delaying this reclamation is pointless, and removing the focus from the addiction also serves to help the addicted individual. As impossible as it may seem, family members can in fact find happiness even while their loved one continues to suffer from his disease.

Chapter Highlights and Suggestions

- Become disentangled from your loved one's addiction

- Reclaim your own life; resume your hobbies, take a vacation, invite friends to your home

- Focus on relationships with other family members

- Consider Al-Anon or professional counseling

- Create a healthy recovery environment free of rescuing

- Encourage personal responsibility in your loved one

SECTION THREE:

HELPING OTHERS

Telling Your Story

Nothing is as powerful as a story. Stories have the power to inform, inspire, and change lives. It's no wonder that Alcoholics Anonymous encourages its members to share their stories, and they normally do so in three parts: what it was like, what happened, and what it's like now. In much the same way, family members can—and should—share their stories.

➤ *What It Was Like*

This portion of the story describes the progressive nature of the suffering brought on by addiction and the personal difficulties experienced by the family member. Shared here are the confusion, shame, denial, and futile efforts to "fix" the loved one. Without attempting to invoke sympathy, the storyteller indicates the growing frustration and eventual decline into a self-defeating course of action that only served to worsen the despair felt by everyone.

Families are impacted by addiction in many of the same ways that the addicted person is affected. Most of the elements of addiction—denial, dishonesty, obsession, boundaries, emotional problems, financial concerns, and loss of reputation—are felt by family members just as they are by their loved one.

For example, denial prevents family members—and their loved one—from accepting the presence of addiction. Embarrassed and ashamed, everyone fervently resists admitting that addiction is the problem.

Denial leads to dishonesty and a family member will first lie to himself. This initial self-deception is normal and centers on what he deeply wants to be true. "He's not really using drugs." "He's getting better." "It's the people he's hanging around with." "He'd never steal from his own family."

Self-deception then progresses to telling actual lies, usually to other family members. The primary rescuer, especially, feels compelled to hoard secrets to protect the loved one from the shame of addiction. Although many areas of the loved one's life are kept secret, financial rescuing is among the most common. Money may be handed surreptitiously to the loved one or his rent might be paid without family knowledge. When other family members become secretive as well, a fragile, complex web of clandestine activities develops which results in multiple hidden alignments with the loved one.

And just as the addicted person becomes obsessed with his drug use, family members become obsessed with their loved one. Personal obligations and the needs of others are neglected. The obsession may reach such intensity that a family member innocently becomes aligned with the addicted loved one in opposition to the rest of the family.

Family members cross personal behavioral boundaries as often as their loved one. A mother, for instance, drove to meet her addicted daughter to give her $500 that was supposedly owed to a drug dealer who had threatened to kill her. A grandmother, under false pretenses, borrowed money from other family members to give to her addicted grandson. Both later remarked, "I never *dreamed* I would have done that!"

Just as addicted people are subject to extreme mood fluctuations, so do family members encounter worrisome episodes of anxiety and depression because of the constant stress caused by the addiction. With progression of the disease, physical health problems emerge and feelings of joylessness and hopelessness compare to those experienced by the addicted person.

We know that addiction can strip the addicted individual of his ability to earn or manage money. Likewise families, intending to be helpful, often spend enormous amounts of money "to solve the problem." Some report spending thousands of dollars more than they can afford on ineffective rescuing. The result is financial instability: second mortgages, depleted retirement accounts, or sale of a car or home appliance.

Loss of reputation occurs both within the family and in the eyes of the community. Struggles with finances, conflicts with family and friends, poor job performance due to distractions, and adversarial attitudes toward law enforcement, courts, and well-intended agencies lead to diminished esteem. Fighting against the world on behalf of their loved one leaves families angry, frustrated, and exhausted.

Family members live with constantly increasing levels of fear and anger. They jump every time the phone rings. "What horrible thing has happened now?" They fear the next crisis. "What will become of the grandchildren?" They dread the next contact with their loved one. "What does he want now?" He'll want some kind of help that shouldn't be given but probably will be given. Fear—both real and imagined—creates a simmering anger that suffocates any inkling of happiness for family members.

➤ *What Happened*

As each addicted person must reach his personal bottom, so must the rescuing family member arrive at a turning point. When overwhelmed by the futility of their actions, family members cry out for a different course of action, another way. Sometimes the family member was aware of an alternative course of action but was not yet ready to try it. Surprisingly often, in the midst of this period of ultimate suffering, a new direction seems to surface spontaneously. But either way the disease of addiction eventually forces family members to "do something different."

> I had tried everything I knew to do to help my son. I had tried most everything over and over again. I knew that money was not the answer and I couldn't stand the thought of bringing him back into my home. I was at a loss, but I also knew that without help I would do the same old thing the same old way and get the same old result. I had attended a meeting of the Loved Ones Group a year before. I'd heard the message, but it seemed too difficult, too harsh. But I was at my bottom. I felt helpless and powerless, but somehow I also felt more open-minded than ever before. There was a feeling of hope in my misery, that perhaps I was ready to accept help and do something different. I loved my son, but I finally realized I wasn't helping him. Instead I was con-

tributing to his progression deeper and deeper into his addiction. It was time to go back to the Loved Ones Group and follow the suggestions.

The path taken by the family often follows the route taken by the addicted loved one. However, when just one family member recognizes that the addiction has been changing everyone's life, a process of recovery can begin. And just as the debilitation caused by the disease of addiction is similar in both family members and those addicted, so too is the recovery process. When family members admit they are powerless over their loved one, an opportunity emerges: they can turn their attention to the impact that the disease has had upon them. The process of breaking through the denial and accepting the truth is a painful but necessary step. When family members stop rescuing and focus on getting better an exciting new story unfolds.

Once a pastor, this father recently shared his story with the Loved Ones Group and then later discussed what he had learned.

My sixteen-year-old son started with prescription medication. In fact, his subsequent drug use consisted entirely of prescription medications, none of which were written for him. He got his first pill at school. He said it made him feel really good, like when I go on long motorcycle rides, only more so.

I was naïve and ignorant for more than two years. I enabled him for sure. I gave him a car, money, and just about whatever he wanted. He began acting a little funny so when I was told that he might be using drugs I searched his room and his car but I didn't find anything. I felt like I wasn't in control. I felt helpless and I didn't like that feeling.

Then checks were missing and we got calls from the bank. I took care of the first bad check; I said it was just a phase he was going through. I was a pastor then and I didn't want things to go public. His brother was furious at me for not turning him in. We tried detox but afterwards he started using again.

I gave him an ultimatum: go to jail or go to treatment. He went to residential treatment. After two months he called me from there and said he was checking himself out and wanted a ride. I drove over and told him he couldn't come home, that there was a homeless shelter four blocks away. He somehow re-mained clean over the weekend and they allowed him back in the treatment place. When he finished treatment I let him come back home. He got his car back and I gave him some money.

Then my mother's bank account was mysteriously overdrawn. The last straw was the call from the bank. I kicked him out. He took his truck and left and spent five nights in his truck. During that time he borrowed a couple of guns from a neighbor "to go target shooting." When he didn't return the guns the neighbor called the sheriff. A warrant was out for his arrest.

Then he called my wife at her workplace. He wanted to leave his truck there and have her take him to jail. He had decided that going to jail was better than living in a truck. He had hit his personal bottom. I told him that two things can happen: "You can go to jail or I can preach at your funeral. I hope you go to jail."

He was locked up for a few days (I was elated and relieved when he was in jail) and then went before the drug court judge who sentenced him to treatment in lieu of incarceration. He was told that if he screwed up in treatment he'd go to jail for eighteen months. When he called home from treatment, I refused to talk to him for a long time. I was angry. When I finally did, near the end of treatment, I said, "You're not coming back home."

He got a job within two days and he's had a job ever since. He was forced to grow up. He's been sober for four years now. When I asked him recently what he thought parents should do when they discover that their child is using drugs he said, "Kick 'em in the ass and don't talk to 'em for a month!"

And here's what this relieved father regularly recommends to Loved Ones Groups:

> *We can get obsessed and consumed by the addiction. I was afraid every time the phone rang: "Is he dead?" We often fail to help ourselves, which would help the addicted person. We need to regain control of our own lives.*

> *You can't lag behind the crises; you've got to get ahead of the curve.*

> *Addicts are all doing the same dance; only the song is different.*

> *They can't recover at home, even after treatment.*

> *No one will change his behavior until he wants to change. The pain must exceed the pleasure of the WOW.*

> *Parents play a big role. We must regain our lives by making the addicted person regain his—by allowing the consequences to happen. Our job is to raise the addict's bottom.*

> *If I could do it over, I'd do something early and harshly.*

You've got to step back—detach—and stop trying to fix everything.

Saying 'no' to even a Happy Meal has power in it.

My wife was supportive. The whole family has to buy into these concepts. Family members must agree ahead to say no if....

I recommend urine testing, even if you're sure he's clean. Kits are available on eBay.

Don't rescue, even after he's in recovery.

The following adult daughter's story illustrates the destructive power of rescuing:

> My parents loved me dearly but their love and my drug addiction nearly killed me. They worked very hard to make sure I had every material thing I could possibly want, within reason. They wanted me to have every opportunity to be successful. They cooperated with all my extracurricular school activities, every special program, and my plan to go to college.
> All that would have been good except that in my junior year of high school I started drinking. At first it was just once in awhile and then it became pretty often. To the alcohol I added marijuana

and then one night I tried a prescription painkiller. As my problems got worse through high school my parents would rescue me from every crisis I created. They even joined me in blaming others for my problems, like hanging around with the wrong friends or unfair teachers. They said my legal problem was just a sign of "a teenager being a teenager."

My parents were divorced and they were also quick to blame each other for my problems. I just let them accept whatever blame they wanted to. By the time I somehow graduated from high school my life was unraveling but I managed to hold things together with the help of my parents.

My maternal grandparents were still living and they had no ability to say 'no' to any of my requests for money or other kinds of help. One weekend when I was high on drugs I wrecked the car that my dad had bought for me. He said he wouldn't give me another. By Monday afternoon my grandparents had provided me with another vehicle. I later wrecked that car too and sold it for drugs.

When I flunked out of college after wasting a lot of my parent's money, they were fed up. Although they allowed me to stay at their homes and eat their food, they'd rarely give me money, so sometimes I stole from them. My mom actually went to see a counselor who told her to cut me off completely, which she pretty much did. When my parents stopped giving me things, my grandfather worked that much harder to help me.

Eventually it was me and Grandpa against the rest of the family. I'd promise him that I'd quit if he'd help me one more time—one more bail, one more rent payment, or one more loan of his car. Finally I could even get him to give me money to buy drugs because he could see how sick I was without them. It hurt my very soul to see him cry and beg me to stop but I couldn't stop. And I couldn't stop promising either.

Toward the end of my drug use my grandfather was paying my rent, buying groceries for me and my addicted boyfriend, paying for both of us to get a daily dose of methadone, and giving us money that we'd use to buy Xanax.

When my boyfriend and I both lost our drivers' licenses, Grandpa drove us back and forth to the methadone clinic, ninety miles round trip, seven days a week. Once I woke up in his car with vomit all over me; I almost choked to death. Two other times I woke up in the emergency room with an irregular heartbeat. My boyfriend thought I was dying.

I don't think Grandpa would ever have been able to say 'no' to me.

But not even Grandpa could rescue me from all my consequences and eventually I was arrested for possession of prescription drugs for which I had no prescription. Grandpa tried to help and he did manage to keep me out of jail. But while on probation I flunked a monthly drug test and ended up in jail anyway. Grandpa's money for the attorney was spent for nothing.

After two more trips to jail for probation violations the court gave me a choice: treatment or prison. At the time this seemed like an easy choice but treatment was very hard to take. Right after I arrived there Grandpa was there too. He gave me money and cigarettes (even though he hated my smoking) and listened to my complaints about the treatment center staff. He even met with the staff to voice my complaints.

The staff saw the problem right away and confronted me about my manipulation. They made it clear that my only chance for recovery was to change my relationship with my grandfather. They threatened to discharge me if I didn't show more interest in the program. Then, somehow, I started to want it and began listening.

It's still very hard. I'm sober but still struggling with life, especially my finances. I live in a housing program sponsored by the treatment agency. Even though I know they're basically the same thing, now I actually find it harder to say 'no' to offers of help from my family than I do saying 'no' to drugs. If I start accepting help from Mom, Dad, or Grandpa it'll only be a matter of time until I start using drugs again.

I have a little job and for the first time in my life I feel like I'm earning what little I have and that feels pretty good. I love my parents and Grandpa but their help is as dangerous to me as my drug use. Hopefully some day I'll be able to have a normal relationship with all of them. Whatever normal is.

➢ *What It's Like Now*

As seen from these stories, when family members recover the story moves into its most powerful part: "What it's like now." This section, more than any other, offers help and hope to others. The concept that people must help others in order to attain and maintain their own recovery—as important as any in this book—has been proven and witnessed on countless occasions. Again and again family members can be heard sharing their stories of change when only recently they were reluctant to even acknowledge the presence of addiction in their family. Once a family member experiences these changes in his own heart and mind, he enthusiastically searches for opportunities to share his story.

Recovery is not achieved without a struggle or emotional pain. While the goal of terminating rescuing behavior is to increase the likelihood that recovery will intervene, the course of events is rarely smooth or predictable. Families often discover that when they successfully abandon their rescuing behaviors and give up their "roles," any "relationship" with their loved one is similarly absent. This most difficult time for families is nonetheless necessary to allow the development of an appropriate, healthy relationship founded on the acceptance of the truth. An unfortunate part of that truth may be the continuation of drug use and downward spiral of their loved one.

Yet once families refrain entirely from contributing monetary and emotional capital to the crises of addiction, they can begin to create a new relationship based on encouragement and love. Family members report with delight that they are happier and feel better physically, have restarted previously enjoyable activities, and have begun to heal strained family relationships. Even while their loved one continues to struggle with his disease, family members can turn their attention toward their own emotional and spiritual progress.

If you're wondering where you can find opportunities to share your own story, you need look no further than your friends, family, co-workers, church members and, if you're lucky, even the occasional stranger. Everywhere and all around you family members are suffering because of the denial, fear, and shame of addiction. Having used the necessary tools and experienced a change, you can have a powerful impact on others simply by sharing the precious gift that personal recovery offers: one's own story.

Through the process of identification, families who have "been there" and experienced the trials of addiction become valuable resources for still-suffering family members. Most family members, and particularly primary rescuers, can identify with the pain and learn of the changes necessary to obtain relief. Paired with the material presented in this book, new ways of looking at and dealing with the loved one become accessible.

But knowing what to do and actually doing it is not the same thing. The apparent abyss between the two can be bridged when newly educated family members hear the stories of those who have accomplished the difficult feat of facing their fears to effectively help their loved one. Like recovering people in AA, families can share their "experience, strength, and hope" with each other and become free to take action.

Equipped with the information in this book and supported by the *Baffled by Addiction?* DVD, small groups of concerned family members can start Loved Ones Groups. In an atmosphere conducive to openness and understanding, families can meet and share their common experiences and discuss the strategies outlined herein. The three groups currently active in our area are making an impressive impact on both families and their addicted loved ones, many of whom were allowed to hit their personal bottoms and enter treatment. The steps involved in creating your own Loved One's Group are available at the *savinglives today.com* website.

As discussed in Chapter 9, Al-Anon is highly recommended not only for family members still in the throes of addiction, but also for those seeking an outlet to help others find the strength to refrain from rescuing by sharing their personal experiences. You can locate groups and find supportive information at *www.al-anon.alateen.org* and *www.al-anonfamilygroups.org.*

Anyone interested in advocacy opportunities should be aware of the serious disconnect between what we know about helping people recover from addiction and how our laws and treatment systems operate. As a nation still fighting the "war on drugs," we are spending most of our resources on interdiction rather than treatment efforts. This has resulted in jails and prisons filled with non-violent addicted people. Even though addiction is at the root of most of our social difficulties, compared to expenditures devoted to other social problems, the resources spent on addiction treatment are miniscule. Much of the resistance to proper allocation rests with addiction's stigma and its effect on the majority of our society. To learn more or become involved in addiction or recovery advocacy, visit *www.facesandvoicesofrecovery.org* and *www.oca-ohio.org.*

The strategies recommended in this book have been developed to resolve the anger that precludes happiness. When family members recognize that addiction is a no-fault condition, cease the rescuing process, and focus instead on love and encouragement, a path is created that leads to the elimination of anger and restoration of the relationship with their loved one, whether or not steps toward recovery have yet been taken.

Remember that addiction is a chronic, lifelong disease. Even after your loved one is safely in recovery he'll have to attend to his condition for the rest of his life. Equally important is the maintenance of a supportive, non-rescuing family environment. Remaining involved in your loved one's life will require continued understanding of both the disease of addiction and the process of recovery.

APPENDICES

A. Symptom Checklist

B. Ten Strategies to Help Your Addicted Loved One

C. The Nature of Addictive Drugs

D. Resources

Texts

DVDs

Organizations and Agencies

Appendix A: Symptom Checklist

To further validate (or invalidate) your suspicions, consider these questions:

- ☐ Has your loved one ever lost time from work due to drinking or drug use?

- ☐ Is your loved one's drinking or drug use making home life unhappy?

- ☐ Does your loved one drink or use drugs because of shyness with other people?

- ☐ Has drinking or drug use ever affected your loved one's reputation?

- ☐ Has your loved one ever expressed remorse after drinking or drug use?

- ☐ Are there any financial difficulties because of your loved one's drinking or drug use?

- ☐ Does your loved one seek an inferior environment when drinking or using drugs?

- ☐ Has your loved one's ambition subsided due to drinking or drug use?

- ☐ Does your loved one ever want a drink or drug in the morning?

☐ Have you noticed less efficiency in your loved one due to drinking or drug use?

☐ Does your loved one sometimes prefer to drink or use drugs alone?

☐ Has a physician ever treated your loved one for drinking or drug use?

☐ Has your loved one ever been hospitalized due to drinking or drug use?

Appendix B: Ten Strategies to Help Your Addicted Loved One

1. **Learn all you can about the disease of addiction.** Obtain information through counseling, open AA and NA meetings, Al-Anon, and Loved Ones Groups.
2. **Don't rescue the addicted individual.** Let him experience the consequences of his disease.
3. **Don't support the addiction financially.** Providing money in any form is rescuing.
4. **Don't analyze the drug use.** Don't try to figure it out or look for underlying causes.
5. **Don't make idle threats, preach, or lecture.** Say what you mean and mean what you say.
6. **Don't extract promises.** An addicted person cannot keep promises.
7. **Avoid the reactions of anger and pity.** Anger eventually leads to pity.
8. **Don't accommodate the disease.** Don't make room for the addiction.
9. **Understand the recovery process.** Relapse is part of the disease.
10. **Reclaim your own life.** Focus on your own joys and responsibilities.

Appendix C: The Nature of Addictive Drugs

History of Addiction

The use of wine and certain narcotics began thousands of years ago and marijuana was used medicinally in China as early as 2700 B.C. Chemical extraction of addictive substances such as morphine, laudanum (tincture of opium) and cocaine began in the nineteenth century. In the early 1900s the unregulated use of opium and morphine yielded addiction estimates of over two hundred thousand individuals.

Legal restraints arose in 1906 with the enactment of the Pure Food and Drug Act, which set standards for drug quality and labeling. The Food, Drug, and Cosmetic Act of 1938 required animal testing and proof of effectiveness. In 1951, the Durham-Humphrey Amendments distinguished between safe, over-the-counter medications and those that require prescriptions for dissemination. Finally, the Controlled Substances Act of 1970 established the Drug Enforcement Agency (DEA) and a list of controlled, or "scheduled," substances.

Controlled Substances

The Controlled Substances Act created five Schedules, or Classes, of drugs based on potential for abuse[*] or dependency and accepted medical uses.

---

[*] the stigmatizing term "abuse" is still used in certain government departments and documents

Schedule or Class	Abuse Potential	Dependency Potential	Medical Use	Examples
I	high	lack of safety	"none"	marijuana, heroin, LSD
II	high	high	approved	morphine, cocaine, oxycodone, meth-amphetamine, some barbiturates
III	moderate	moderate	approved	hydrocodone, codeine, benzo-diazepines, some barbiturates, anabolic steroids
IV	low	limited	approved	some barbiturates
V	low	minimal	approved	antitussives, antidiarrheals (limited narcotic amounts)

Addictive Drugs

Seen in another perspective, the following table includes nicotine and alcohol, which are not scheduled drugs, but addictive and legal nonetheless. Also referenced in the table are brand names and some of the more common "street" names. Note that many scheduled drugs are not solely street drugs and may be obtained through prescription and pharmaceutical sources.

Addictive Substance	Schedule/ Class	Brand Names	Street Names
Nicotine	--	numerous tobacco products	smokes, fags, butts
Opioids: heroin	I	none	smack, junk, dope, horse, skunk, brown sugar
oxycodone	II	*Oxycontin* (continuous release) *Percodan*(+ASA) *Percocet, Tylox* (+acetaminophen)	
hydrocodone	III	*Lortab, Lorcet, Vicodin* (+acetaminophen)	
Cocaine	II		coke, snow, nose candy, flake, blow, big C, lady, snowbirds, white crack
crack cocaine			
Alcohol	--	numerous products	booze, hooch
Methamphetamine	II	none	snorted: speed, crystal injected: crank smoked: ice, glass
Benzodiazepines	III	*Xanax, Valium, Librium*	benzos, downers

| Barbiturates | II, III, IV | *Nembutal, Seconal, Amytal, Tuinal* | downers, yellow jackets, goof balls, red devils |
| Marijuana | I | none | pot, grass, weed, bud, dope, hydro, nails, blunts |

Addiction in the United States

Despite regulation and enforcement, both the use of illegal drugs and the illegal use of legal drugs (underage drinking and smoking) flourish in this country. Today most people live with or know of at least one individual impacted by drugs or alcohol. In the United States, estimates for alcoholism range from fifteen to nineteen million people; for drugs the estimates are between three and four million.

The following table indicates that in the U.S., 22.3 million people are addicted to drugs or alcohol, representing 9.2% of the population.

Substance	U.S. Addicts or Abusers (millions)	Percent of population
Alcohol	18.7	7.7%
Drugs	3.6	1.5%
Tobacco	71.5	29%
Caffeine	194-219	80-90%

(Adapted from *Time*, July 16, 2007)

Individual Drugs

The following descriptions of the more common addictive drugs provide additional understanding of the characteristics of each.

➤ *Alcohol*

The type of alcohol found in alcoholic beverages is ethyl alcohol, or ethanol. No matter that it's beer, wine, or liquor—they all contain ethanol. The claim, "I can't be an alcoholic; I only drink beer," is an obvious falsehood.

Compared to other drugs, alcohol is relatively inexpensive, so life problems associated with its use are less commonly financial. And while ingesting moderate amounts of alcohol may be beneficial in selected individuals, more than a daily intake of two beers, a glass of wine, or a shot of spirits may mean that the use has become a problem.

Technically classified as a sedative, alcohol is better known for its immediate, stimulant effects. The early symptoms of alcohol ingestion are well known: giddiness, loss of inhibitions, pathognomonic breath odor, bizarre judgment, sloppiness, double vision, and delayed reaction time.

The long-term excessive intake of alcohol produces devastating health problems. Liver disease is most common; alcoholic hepatitis may progress to alcoholic cirrhosis. Other conditions related to alcoholism include heart disease, hypertension, stroke, cancer, and pancreatitis.

Like the withdrawal seen with benzodiazepines, sudden abstinence after a period of heavy, sustained drinking can result in life-threatening symptoms. During the first twelve hours of cessation, minor withdrawal effects, such as anxiety, sweating, tremors, and heart palpitations cause discomfort.

More marked symptoms may follow and produce severe dysfunction. These phenomena include alcoholic hallucinosis, which may present as visual, auditory, or tactile hallucinations; generalized withdrawal seizures; and alcohol withdrawal delirium (delirium tremens, or DTs), which manifests as disorientation, hallucinations, elevated blood pressure, fever, and sweating.

Indications for hospitalization (inpatient detoxification) for an individual experiencing alcoholic withdrawal, as recommended by the American Academy of Family Physicians are as follows: prior history of severe withdrawal symptoms, history of seizures or DTs, multiple prior detoxifications, coexisting psychiatric or medical illness, recent heavy alcohol consumption, pregnancy, or lack of satisfactory social support.

➤ *Opioids*

Opioids are addictive analgesics (pain-relievers) and many are prescription narcotics.

Heroin is a highly addictive, illegal opiate synthesized from morphine obtained from opium poppies. The white powder sold in 100 milligram "bags" on the street is usually reduced in purity by the addition of starch, powdered milk, or quinine. Until the recent increase in heroin purity, the substance was dissolved and injected via intravenous, subcutaneous, or intramuscular routes. Now users often snort (inhale) or smoke the powder, which not only produces an immediate, intense high, but also reduces the risk of hepatitis and HIV from contaminated syringes and needles. Heroin is a Class I scheduled narcotic with no approved medical applications. Symptoms of toxicity include labored breathing, blue nails and lips, muscle spasticity, weak pulse, delirium, and coma.

Oxycodone, a Class II narcotic with high addiction potential, is prescribed as Oxycontin (continuous release), Percodan (oxycodone plus aspirin), and Percocet or Tylox (oxycodone plus acetaminophen). Some Oxycontin users chew and swallow the tablets. For a more rapid high seriously addicted individuals crush the tablets and snort the powder or dissolve the powder in water and inject the solution. Overdose symptoms include slow breathing, constricted pupils, loss of consciousness, and coma.

Hydrocodone, a slightly less addictive Class III drug, appears as Lortab, Lorcet, and Vicodin, which contain acetaminophen as an additive. The uses and symptoms associated with hydrocodone are similar to oxycodone.

> *Cocaine*

Classified as a stimulant, cocaine is derived from the leaves of the coca plant. After receiving multi-kilogram shipments from producing countries, wholesalers break down the powder into gram-size bags, which are retailed on the street by drug dealers.

Injection and snorting routes are used, but the most immediate and intense high is obtained by smoking the drug. This highly addictive Class II narcotic is used medically only for topical anesthesia in eye and nasal surgery. Hyperthermia, hallucinations, and convulsions are noted overdose symptoms.

Crack cocaine is produced by boiling cocaine powder in a solution of sodium bicarbonate or ammonia and water; the solid residue is then dried and broken up into roughly half-gram "rocks." Because crack is relatively inexpensive and produces an explosive high when smoked, the substance remains a popular drug of choice. As with most drugs, smoking crack results in increased compulsive drug-seeking.

> ➤ *Methamphetamine*

Another powerful stimulant and closely related chemically to amphetamine, methamphetamine appears in the drug-seeking community as meth powder, crystal meth ("ice"), and meth tablets. Clandestine "meth labs" manufacture methamphetamine from ephedrine or pseudoephedrine found in cold medications. Since additional toxic chemicals, such as isopropyl alcohol, toluene, sulfuric acid or phosphorus, are required for its production, devastating side effects are common.

The rush after smoking crystal meth occurs almost immediately and, because it is metabolized more slowly than crack cocaine, lasts for several hours. Meth binges, lasting a week or two with little sleep, often end with "tweaking," where the user is intensely paranoid. Tweakers, who often become involved in domestic disputes, motor vehicular accidents and burglaries, must be handled with caution; their edgy irritability hides a constant threat of violence.

Many of the long-term effects of prolonged meth use are irreversible and include cognitive dysfunction, memory loss, tooth decay and loss, constant skin scratching, twitching, speech disorders, panic attacks, and seizures.

➤ *Benzodiazepines*

The benzodiazepine drugs, which are Class III depressants, act as sedatives in low doses, tranquilizers in moderate doses, and hypnotics at high doses. They are widely prescribed and include brand names such as Xanax, Valium, and Librium.

Benzodiazepine usage is supported by multi-doctor prescribing, forged prescriptions, and diverted, illicit pharmaceutical sources. Because use is particularly high among heroin and cocaine users, a significant percentage of individuals entering treatment for these addictions must be carefully observed for benzodiazepine withdrawal which, like withdrawal from alcohol and barbiturates, can be life-threatening.

➤ *Barbiturates*

Classified as sedative-hypnotics, barbiturates fall into Classes II, III, and IV, depending on individual drug dependency potential. Intoxication with Class II drugs, such as pentobarbital (Nembutal), secobarbital (Seconal), amobarbital (Amytal) and an amobarbital-secobarbital combination (Tuinal), produces an alcohol-like euphoria; symptoms mimic alcohol intoxication.

Because drug tolerance is attained rapidly and because the therapeutic-to-toxic range is narrow, overdose is common. High doses can result in nervous and respiratory system depression, coma, and death. Also, like alcohol and benzodiazepines, withdrawal may be life-threatening and must be medically supervised.

> ➤ *Marijuana*

Marijuana, a Class I controlled drug, is the world's most widely used illegal substance. Derived from the plant *Cannabis sativa*, the active ingredient in marijuana is the cannabinoid THC (delta-9-tetrahydrocannabinol). By far most marijuana is smoked as a rolled cigarette ("joint"), in a hollowed-out cigar ("blunt"), or in a pipe ("bong"). Some users ingest the drug laced in brownies or cookies. Synthetic THC is available medically in the pill Marinol to relieve the nausea associated with chemotherapy and the anorexia seen in AIDS patients.

The immediate effects of inhaled marijuana include impaired memory, concentration, and judgment; loss of balance and coordination; increased heart rate; blood shot eyes; and increased appetite (the "munchies").

Common long-term effects of marijuana are psychological addiction, physical withdrawal symptoms, paranoia, anxiety, and impaired learning and memory skills. Compared to cigarettes, marijuana smoke contains four times the level of tar and fifty to seventy percent more carcinogenic hydrocarbons and thus may increase the risk of lung cancer.

The Chemistry of Addiction

An exhaustive review of the physiological aspects of addiction is beyond the scope of this book, but a brief overview will help to establish further that addiction is a disease of the body. The pleasure centers in the human brain are impacted at the molecular level by ingested addictive substances just as they are by our natural hormones. Laboratory and clinical breakthroughs being made at an astounding rate are unraveling the complex pathways involved in chemically induced human behavior. Brain imaging technology, for example, has already identified the physical locations for many human behavioral responses to drugs, and ongoing genetic studies are revealing fundamental differences in the metabolism of addiction-prone individuals.

Ethanol, the type of alcohol found in alcoholic beverages, is first absorbed by the stomach and upper small intestine. While ten percent is eliminated unchanged through the lungs and urine, ninety percent is metabolized in the liver. The enzymatic breakdown of ethanol is as follows:

$$\text{ethanol} \xrightarrow{\text{ADH}} \text{acetaldehyde} \xrightarrow{\text{ALDH}} \text{acetate} + CO_2 + H_2O$$

ADH = alcohol dehydrogenase
ALDH = aldehyde dehydrogenase

Ethanol is converted to acetaldehyde by the enzyme alcohol dehydrogenase. The adverse side effects, such as nausea, headache, dizziness and fatigue, are caused by the accumulation of acetaldehyde in the body. Acetaldehyde then shows up in the brain as opiate-like substances called tetraisoquinolines, or TIQs. These "false neurotransmitters" activate the brain's pleasure centers and cause intense emotional gratification. The enzyme aldehyde dehydrogenase then converts acetaldehyde to harmless acetate, carbon dioxide, and water.

Drugs also affect the brain's pleasure centers. Normally dopamine, the naturally occurring chemical that activates these centers, is released by the brain in response to food, sex, and other enjoyable activities. Substances that affect the amount of dopamine available lead to exaggerated responses. The arrival of amphetamines in the brain, for example, elevates the amount of dopamine released which, in turn, stimulates the pleasure centers. Cocaine blocks the reabsorption, or reuptake, of dopamine thereby increasing the amount available. Heroin and morphine act by blocking the release of GABA (gamma-aminobutyric acid), a dopamine inhibitor normally responsible for regulating dopamine's effects. No matter the exact mode of action, the effect is the same: flooding the brain's pleasure centers with excess amounts of a chemical (dopamine) to produce an explosive WOW experience.

Appendix D: Resources

Texts:

Alcoholics Anonymous ("The Big Book"), Chapter 9: "The Family Afterward," Alcoholics Anonymous World Services, Inc., 1939

Alcoholism: The Genetic Inheritance, by Kathleen W. Fitzgerald, Ph.D., Whales' Tale Press, 2002

Courage to Change: One Day at a Time in Al-Anon II, Al-Anon Family Group Headquarters, Inc., 1992

One Day at a Time in Al-Anon, Al-Anon Family Group Headquarters, Inc., 1978

The Addictive Personality: Understanding the Addictive Process and Compulsive Behavior, by Craig Nakken, Hazelden, 1996

The Selfish Brain: Learning from Addiction, by Robert L. Dupont, M.D., Hazelden, 1997

Under the Influence: A Guide of the Myths and Realities of Alcoholism, by James R. Milam, Ph.D., and Katherine Ketcham, Bantam Books, 1981

DVDs:

Addiction, HBO, 2007

Baffled by Addiction? A Seven Part Series for Loved Ones, The Counseling Center, Inc., Portsmouth, OH, available at www. savinglivestoday.com

Organizations & Agencies:

Al-Anon: www.al-anon.alateen.org; www. al-anonfamilygroups.org

Alcoholics Anonymous: www.alcoholics-anonymous.org

National Drug Court Institute: www.ndci.org

The Counseling Center, Inc., Portsmouth, OH: www.thecounselingcenter.org

Recovery advocacy: www.facesandvoicesofrecovery. org www.oca-ohio.org

INDEX

Bold page numbers indicate major topic sections

Notes

CPSIA information can be obtained
at www.ICGtesting.com
Printed in the USA
LVHW101129200522
719207LV00002B/256